Bicycling Greater Vancouver and the Gulf Islands

PHOTOGRAPHS
Maggie Burtinshaw
Mary Ellen Bradshaw

TEXT
Mary Ellen Bradshaw
Maggie Burtinshaw

MAPS
Susan Pritchard of Rabbit designs

Second Printing 1990

Canadian Cataloguing in Publication Data
Bradshaw, Mary Ellen
Burtinshaw, Maggie
Bicycling Greater Vancouver and the Gulf Islands
ISBN 0-9692330-0-0

Printed in Canada by:
Hignell Printing Limited
Winnipeg, Canada

Distributed by
Gordon Soules Book publisher
Vancouver

The authors take no responsibility for Road conditions, Ferry schedules,
Museum hours etc. as they are subject to change.

Acknowledgements

Our sincere thanks to the many people and organizations that helped us with this project.

Special thanks to:

Gordon Soules

Jack Hignell

Ruth Hoyem

Paul Crozier

Loris Talmey

Julie Burtinshaw

Cynthia Burtinshaw

Jenifer Crombie

Gina Lucas

Jim Dorman

Peter Bradshaw

Susan and Gordon Pritchard

Karen Kelm of B.C. Parkways (ALRT)

Christy Illic of B.C. Parkways (ALRT)

Richmond Leisure Services

Richmond Visitor's and Convention Bureau

B.C. Tourism Ministry

Foreword

This book came about because my friend Maggie and I decided it was time to take a long look at fitness and health. We chose cycling because it seemed a lot more interesting than the many alternative forms of exercise. Cycling, we could cover a lot more territory than if we walked or ran, and at 13 miles per hour, cycling burns 680 calories, which is considerably more than walking (200-300), tennis (400-500) or Golf (250).

As our fitness and stamina increased we wished to expand our biking horizons. Besides, we became bored with the same old scenery. In search of newer, greener pastures, we looked for a biking book to guide us in our quest. We didn't want to climb mountains or ride a 100 miles in a stretch. We wanted a guide for the recreational cyclist: Short morning rides before work, bike picnics, afternoon, and even some full day and over-night trips. We wanted to know the bike trails, country lanes and parks where a family could spend a pleasant Sunday together. We couldn't find such a book, so we overhauled our bikes and set about to explore greater Vancouver and the Gulf Islands. Then we wrote about it.

In the process we improved our physical well-being, and two born and bred Vancouverites rediscovered the region in which we live. Not only did we learn a great deal about our B.C. heritage and history, during our many visits to the excellent local museums, historical sites and landmarks, but more importantly, we had a lot of fun. With **"Bicycling Greater Vancouver and the Gulf Islands,"** we'd like to share that fun with you.

Mary Ellen Bradshaw
Maggie Burtinshaw

Table of contents

8

Introduction

A Little Bit of History

The earliest existing trace of man and wheeled, self-propulsion is on a stained glass, church window in Stokes Poges, Buckinghamshire, England. This shows a figure sitting on a wheeled device, using his feet on the ground for propulsion. Later, during the seventeen hundreds, many ponderous and inefficient models were developed. These were mostly used as novelties, and were so expensive to make, that only the upper classes could afford them.

The first pedal bicycle was developed in Scotland in 1840, and the inventor, Kirkpatrick MacMillan, was once prosecuted and fined for "furious driving." This model was improved by Gavin Dalzel in 1846, and was followed by the "Boneshaker" built by a Frenchman, Pierre Lallement. It was so called, because of the way it vibrated on the rough roads.

Many other models followed, including, the "Ordinary" and the "Safety". Since then, intensive research and development has resulted in the finely crafted, efficient machines we have today.

Bicycle Touring

Bicycle touring has been popular in Europe for decades, particularly in Germany, England, France, Holland, Italy, Belgium and Denmark. In the last ten years, interest in cycling has increased in the U.S. and Canada. This is due to the energy crisis, resulting in higher gasoline prices, and the renewed interest in fitness and health.

Map Legend

BRIDGE

BIKE ROUTE

OTHER ROADS

BICYCLE SHOP

FERRY

CAMPSITE

Rules of the Road and safety hints

- Ride with motor traffic not against it
- Do not ride on a sidewalk unless otherwise directed by a sign
- Yield to pedestrians
- Ride as near as practicable to the right side of the roadway
- Do not ride abreast of another person on a roadway (Single file only)
- Keep at least one hand on the handlebars
- Listen carefully at all times (Do not wear earphones, walkman's)
- Maintain safe speed
- Exercise caution in congested areas
- Be alert to highway signs
- Do not double
- Watch out for doors being opened by persons in cars parked along the roadway.
- Every bicycle must be equipped with a warning bell. Use bell for warning of your approach.
- At night, a bright front light visible to at least 150 meters and a large red reflector on unobscured location on the back of the bike are required by law.
- Always look behind before you change direction. Signal before turning.
- If confronted by a ferocious dog, jump off your bike on the side opposite to the dog, and use the bike as a shield.
- Check with Cycling association for info regarding restrictions and regulations regarding cycling on Bridges.

Bicycling Association of B.C.
1200 Hornby Street
Vancouver, B.C. V6Z 2E2   Phone: (604) 559-Bike

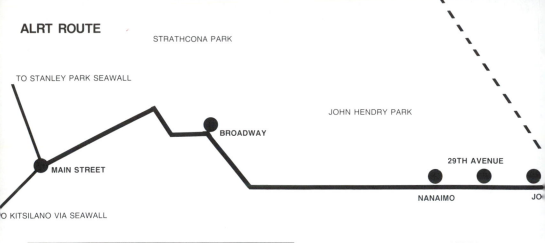

ALRT ROUTE

STRATHCONA PARK

TO STANLEY PARK SEAWALL

JOHN HENDRY PARK

BROADWAY

MAIN STREET

29TH AVENUE

O KITSILANO VIA SEAWALL

NANAIMO   JO

VANCOUVER

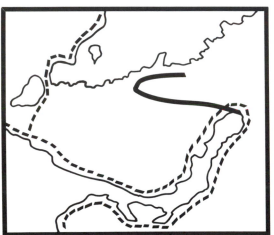

The British Columbia Parkway cycle Path*

19 km / 12 miles

Terraine: 2 metre wide asphalt path

Funded by private enterprise, individual citizens and three levels of government, **the British Columbia Parkway is a 19 kilometre (12 mile) linear park, parelleling the Vancouver Regional Rapid Transit System, through Vancouver, Burnaby and New Westminster.** Along the route, Side-by-side, there will be a two metre wide asphalt, bike path (thanks to a 600,000.00 dollar donation from 7-11 Stores,) and a crushed limestone or cinder walking and jogging path. **It will eventually connect the waterfront at False Creek, to the Fraser river in New Westminster,**

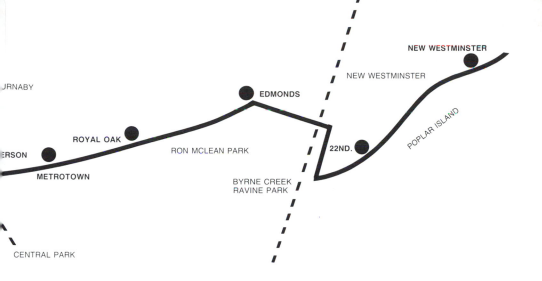

joining 32 existing parks. There are also plans for this path to eventually meet up with the Kitsilano and Stanley Park seawalls, via extensions of the seawalls through B.C. Place. Other park trails already proposed by the respective municipalities could also tie into this system.

The route starts at Main Street Station. As you ride down the landscaped path, you will pass miles of flowers and trees donated or paid for by private individuals, groups and the business community. You'll marvel at the stand of white dogwoods, donated by the Van Dusen gardens. Perhaps you'll reflect a moment, while passing the mile of red tulips donated by members of the Canadian legion, to honour the veterans of two wars. There may be an international mile of flags, fountains, and ethnic plazas, where cultural events could take place. Along the route there will be water fountains, picnic grounds, waterparks and playgrounds. There will be fitness stations, exercise aids and benches to rest. There could even be a miniature village and an outdoor sculpture gallery. **The route ends at New Westminster station.**

The parkway will be lit by adjacent street lighting and where necessary, by decorative lamp standards. Near intersection entry points, traffic bollards will be installed for safety. ***This unique concept in recreational planning will be completed in March of 1986.**

As an added note: The bike path will not only be a boon for the recreational cyclist but will provide a safe, pleasant route for those who wish to avoid the crush of cars in the rush hour traffic. What better than an invigorating ride to the office first thing in the morning?

13

VANCOUVER

In 1889, Lord Stanley stood on the heights of Prospect Point and dedicated one thousand acres of parkland "to the use and enjoyment of people of all colours, creeds and customs for all time. I name thee Stanley Park." We are fortunate in Vancouver to have such a unique and natural forested area within walking and cycling distance of the city centre. It is one of the many and varied routes we have to offer both the cycling tourist and local bikers.

Our hope is that as time goes by, with more and more people becoming aware of the joys of cycling, that the motoring public will accept us as partners on the road. Riding a bicycle is no longer simply a recreation, but has become a welcome alternate mode of transportation. Obeying the rules of the road is vital in a high traffic area such as downtown Vancouver. In order to enjoy your ride with safety, we urge you to respect all traffic signals and to proceed with caution. We are all emmisaries in helping the general public and local governments to accept us on equal terms with motorists.

Enjoy our local rides with your friends and family, as you cycle an historic tour of the city centre, Chinatown and Gastown, where our beautiful city was born, or enjoy an opportunity to pedal through some of our most attractive residential districts. Here you will see a profile of Vancouver that the ordinary tourist never finds. If you live here, there are some surprises in store for you! These are rides for the whole family, with wonderful picnic stops along the way. Our very first ride, THE BRITISH COLUMBIA PARKWAY, follows the ALRT line and is an example of the new acceptance by government of bicycling needs. When completed, it will offer a delightful, protected family tour and fast, safe ride for the commuter from New Westminster to downtown Vancouver.

BE CAUTIOUS! BE SAFE! ENJOY!

**Kits Point
U.B.C.
Southlands
Shaughnessy**

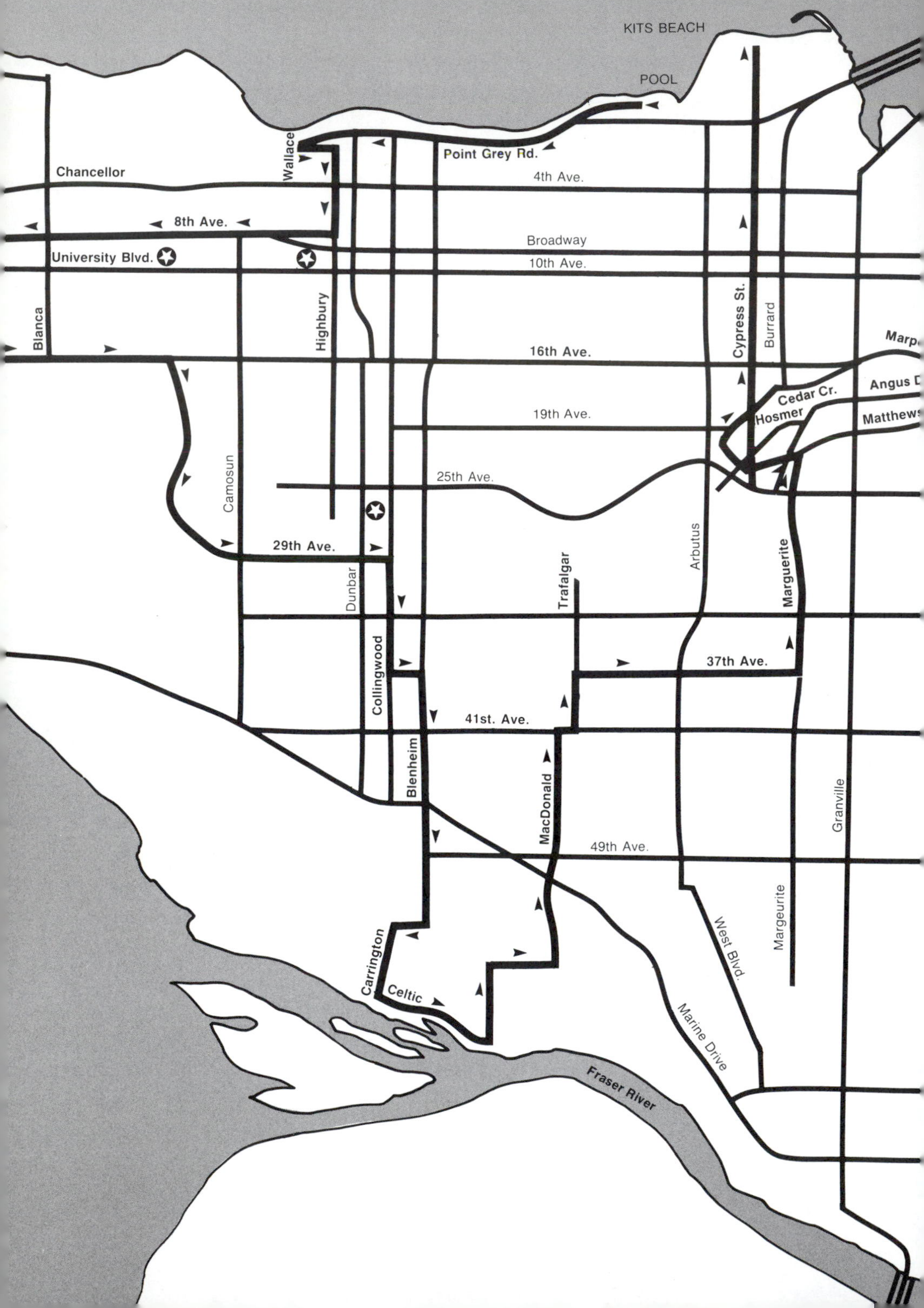

KITS BEACH

POOL

Wallace

Point Grey Rd.

Chancellor

4th Ave.

8th Ave.

Broadway

University Blvd.

10th Ave.

Blanca

Highbury

Cypress St.

Burrard

Marpe

16th Ave.

Cedar Cr.

Angus D

19th Ave.

Hosmer

Matthews

Camosun

25th Ave.

Arbutus

Marguerite

29th Ave.

Dunbar

Trafalgar

Collingwood

37th Ave.

Blenheim

41st Ave.

Granville

MacDonald

49th Ave.

Marguerite

West Blvd.

Carrington

Celtic

Marine Drive

Fraser River

City Route #1
Kits. Point-U.B.C.-Southlands-Shaughnessy

36km/22 miles

Terrain: paved roads, paved bicycle paths, and a few small hills.

From Kitsilano Beach, take the marked bicycle route along Point Grey Road, which starts above the Kitsilano Yacht Club and directly west of the large outdoor, seawater pool. If an early morning dip suits you, pool hours are 7:00 A.M.-8:45 P.M. from May 24th to the Labour Day weekend. **This section of Point Grey Road, which dips below busy Cornwall, is only three blocks long,** and is serenely quiet. There are still a few of the original old Kits. mansions amongst the modern condominiums. **Bearing left at the end of this unique street** you will see a small green space which gives access to a fine view of the opposite shore. There are steps here to the rocky beach below. **Continue right (west) along Point Grey Road following the sea.** The bicycle route is well posted along the way and takes you past a number of beautiful homes, interspersed with parks, offering glimpses of the ocean and mountains. A small museum, The Old Hastings Mill, sits on a grassy slope at Alma and Point Grey Road, overlooking the Royal Vancouver Yacht Club. The small frame structure is the oldest building in Vancouver and was originally located at the foot of Dunlevy Street, on the waterfront, where it was the General Store for the Hastings Mill. Visiting hours are 10:00-4:00 daily. **Staying on Point Grey Road, cycle west past the R.V.Y.C. and the Jericho Tennis Club** and further along to Tudor style Brock House which was designed by Samuel McLure, an architect famous in that era for a number of beautiful manor houses in Vancouver.

To follow the marked bike route, backtrack from Brock House to Wallace Street and jog right and then immediately left on 1st Avenue as far as Highbury Street, turning right through a residential area of small, attractive homes.

Dismount and walk the bicycles across busy Fourth Avenue, continuing south along Highbury. Turning right at 8th Avenue will take you up the hill past the Jericho Military Base and on the rise of the hill, the Jericho Hill School for the Deaf. The original buildings on this site housed a juvenile correctional centre. At that time it was in the wilderness, which was a deterrent to runaways, the forest being full of dangerous, wild animals, such as bear, cougar and wolves.

The road **jogs to the left and then to the right at the junction of West Broadway and 8th Avenue.** Two blocks to the south of 8th and Trimble is the beginning of the shopping district of the University. There are many small boutiques, restaurants, bookstores and a cinema. If you're hungry, try the University Bakery, famous in Vancouver for its sourdough bread.

Opposite the University Endowment Lands at 8th and Blanca, turn left. Turn right at University Boulevard (Tenth Avenue riding into U.B.C., past THE GATES. Here is the start of a genuine bicycle path which takes you past the greens of the University Golf Course. Points of interest are marked on the inset map of the university.

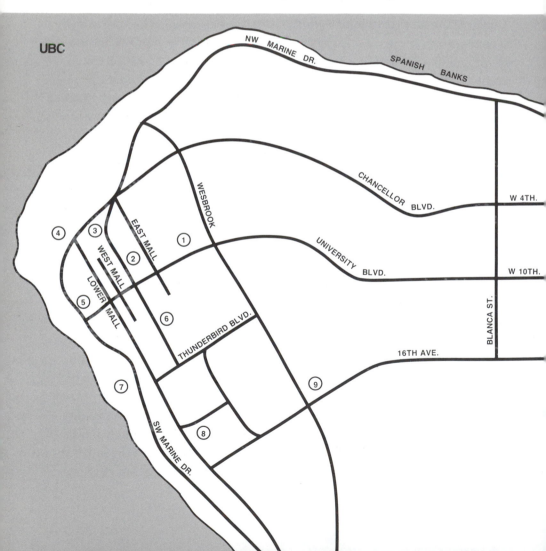

EXIT:

Take Westbrook Mall south to 16th Avenue. Turn left (east) along the protected bicycle path to Imperial Drive. Turn right (south-east) through the woods past St. George's Senior School at 29th Avenue and Comosun Street. **Continuing along 29th Avenue** will take you past the residence and junior school, which is housed in one of Vancouver's finest old buildings. Until recent years it was the Convent of the Sacred Heart Private School for Girls. At Dunbar Street there are a number of small shops if you are in need of refreshments. **Dismount and cross Dunbar Street, continuing along 29th Avenue to Collingwood, turning right (south) and then left (east) onto 37th Avenue.** This is mainly a through street to **Blenheim, where you will turn right (south), finally crossing busy 41st Avenue.** Passing Crofton House Private School for Girls on the left **descend to 49th Avenue, crossing this street at the intersection light.**

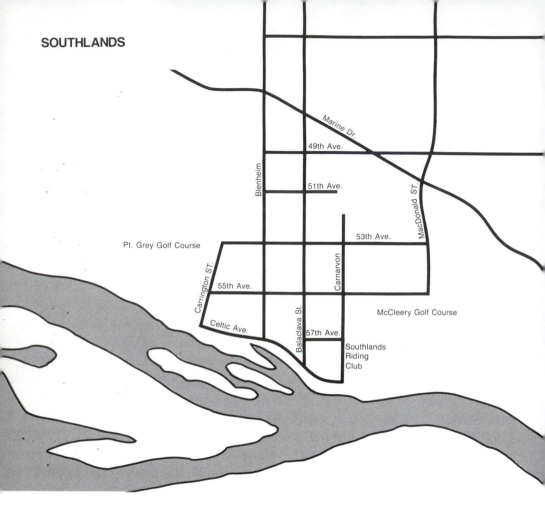

You are now entering an area that would be unique in any large city — a small pocket of country within the city limits: **the Southlands Flats. Travelling south down the hill** we will pass the wide green expanse of the Point Grey Golf Course, **eventually turning right at 53rd Avenue to Carrington and on down to the Fraser River,** where the Celtic Shipyards are located. **Between Blenheim to the west, Celtic to the south, MacDonald to the east and 49th to the north, here is the world of horses!** Any of these delightful country lanes will take you past magnificent animals, or perhaps some young children will ride along proudly beside you on their well-groomed ponies. It is a perfect place for a leisurely family cycle and is without exception flat and easy to ride. **Be sure to meander down the tiny horse-lined lane of Prescott Street.** To leave the Southlands area **proceed north on MacDonald Street past the Southlands Riding and Polo Club and the McCleery Public Golf Course to 49th Avenue. Walking your bicycles across Marine Drive and 49th**

Avenue would be wise as the traffic moves very quickly here. **Continue north up the hill to 41st Avenue, turning right (east) to Trafalgar.** A few blocks further east along 41st Avenue are the shops of Kerrisdale, one of Vancouver's best shopping districts. **To continue the route, turn left and cross the road, riding north to 37th Avenue. Then turn right, (east) where you can continue with your journey into the rarified reaches of Shaughnessy, Vancouver's wealthiest residential district.**

SHAUGHNESSY

37th Avenue will eventually lead to Marguerite Street, in the heart of Shaughnessy. This land was owned by the Canadian Pacific Railway and cleared for subdividing in 1908. **Turn left** and ride along tranquil, tree-lined streets until you come upon Vancouver's most fascinating, old mansion **at the corner of Marguerite and Matthews:** Glen Brae, which means "valley by the mountains" in Gaelic. You will be taken back to Victorian times when you see this turreted and ornate house surrounded by its unusual wrought iron fence of thistles, the national flower of Scotland. This fence, manufactured in Scotland, to remind its owner of his native land, originally had gold-leaf rosettes as part of its design. William Lamont Tait, a lumber and Real Estate tycoon, had his home built high on a ridge so as to capture the then unobstructed view of Vancouver. The twin cupulas distinguish it from any other house in Vancouver, and each has ten arched windows, with stained glass along the curve of the arches. The ballroom floor was laid over a padding of seaweed to give it spring. It is now a home for wealthy seniors, and we might see a pale face peeking from the third floor windows, where once there was a glittering array of dancers gliding by to the sound of music and laughter.

From the corner of Matthews and Marguerite go left (west) on Matthews and right (east) on Angus Drive, following the wide boulevard around to the first or second opening in the road after Alexandra. Turn left and double back to Hosmer. This will take you past many stately homes and the spacious boulevard in the Centre is a great spot for a rest and a snack. **Turn right on Hosmer** which will start you on the gradual descent back to Kitsilano Beach. **At the junction of Cedar Crescent, Cypress Street and 19th Avenue the quiet, shady crescents of Shaughnessy are left behind. Turn right on Cypress, around the roundabout and continue north down the hill on this safer side street, until crossing Cornwall Avenue to Kits. Point and the end of this delightful city tour.**

City Tour #2
Kits Point, Granville Island, False Creek

10 km/6.2 miles

Terrain: Paved roads and paths

Points of Interest:
1. Kits Showboat: nightly family entertainment Sea Festival July 17th-21st and until mid-August. Free
2. One hundred foot Centennial Totem Pole, an exact replica of the one carved for Queen Elizabeth II, by Chief Mungo Martin of the KWAKIUTL NATION. Each figure on the pole represents one of the mythical creatures of the ten tribes of these famous west coast indians.
3. Vancouver Maritime Museum, with the Royal Canadian Mounted Police Arctic Patrol Vessel, the St. Roch, landlocked in the soaring glass and cedar building. Winter hours: 10:00 A.M.-5:00 P.M. Summer hours: 10:00 A.M.-6:00 P.M.
4. Heritage Ship Harbour
5. Ferry trips to Granville Island Market

This short and easy family bicycle tour Begins at Kitsilano Beach, a favourite meeting place and sunspot for Vancouverites. It is named after a descendant of the legendary Chief Khaatsa-lah-nogh.

From the west end of the seawater pool at Point Grey Road and to Cornwall Street you will see the beginning of the marked bicycle route along the edge of the park. (1)

Follow the path, bearing down to the left and right across the parking lot to Arbutus Street. Turn left past the playing fields. From the rise of the slight incline, you can view the panorama of the moutains of West Vancouver and as far along as the Sunshine Coast. Usually there are a number of foreign freighters standing to in the harbour, waiting permission to enter the Port of Vancouver. **Turn right on McNicoll and left on Maple Street** past the cool, tree-shaded grassy slope leading to the crest of the hill, where washroom facilities are located. **With a right turn at Ogden,** you have a fine view of English Bay and the high rise apartment towers across the water. (2,3,4,5) **Turn left on Chestnut to the sea path which hugs the bay as far as the boat launch.**

Directly in front of us is the Burrard Street Bridge, and beyond that, the Granville Street Bridge. It is under the latter, that the Granville Market is located. **Continue on the marked bicycle route, past the Vancouver Archives, the Planetarium, and the Vancouver Academy of Music.** There is an unofficial path to the left, which leads to a short cut under the Burrard Street Bridge, and then directly to the market, but **the posted route continues to Chestnut Street where you turn left, then right on Cornwall, and left again on Cypress Street to 1st Avenue. Turning left here** will take you past (or into!) one of the finest bakeries of French bread in Vancouver: The Bread Garden. They are also popular for their buttery, melt-in-your-mouth croissant and cappuccino coffee. **Dismount to cross busy Burrard Street continuing on 1st Avenue** — past art and woodworking studios and The Stone Carver's Workshop. **Bear left over the tracks, and then bear right around the front of the new apartment buildings to the cycling path and along the seawall.** You will ride alongside one of the many marinas in this area before you **turn to the left on Anderson** will take you to Granville Island and the market. **Turn right on Cartwright, following the one way route, which winds its way around the island.**

There are many attractions to please the visitor in this renovated industrial site, such as glassblowing demonstrations, the music of the steel drums, guitars, flutes and harps or watch the jugglers on the pier and be serenaded by a quartet playing renaissance music. There are boutiques, restaurants, bookstores and a fine French Patisserie and Charcouterie, along with the Market itself, which boasts the best of local and imported natural and gourmet foods. There is something for every palate and interest. You can sit on the dock in front of the market to eat lunch, or you can just sun yourself and watch the spectacular yachts motor by.

If you wish to tour the False Creek residential side of the waterway, ride back along Anderson and turn left, and follow Park Way. On the periphery of the Island, there are special areas for children: the water pond as you cross Anderson to Park Way, and the popular children's water park, behind Isadora's Family Restaurant, also to the left. **Continue on this path, winding your way around the waters of False Creek,** with B.C. Place, the site of the World Exposition on Transportation and Communications, Expo'86, just across the tranquil waters on the left (north). Providing a splendid backdrop to the Expo'86 site are the coastal mountains. On the right, (south) are the many and varied architectually styled apartments and condominiums. Interspersed with these are the open, sunny areas as well as the tree-shaded ponds and parks, the community school and children's playground.

Ahead as you ride along the bicycle path, there is an excellent view of the phenomenal, 17 storey Geodesic Dome, the Expo Centre, at the east end of False Creek, so called by Captain George Vancouver, when he discovered that he was not sailing up a river, but rather a short inlet. In this sparkling centrepiece will be shown spectacular images on the giant Omnimax Theatre screen. Famous and popular shows and exhibits, as well as excellent restaurants and high profile entertainment will be part of the attraction of the unusual Expo Centre.

Just before the end of the route, you'll arrive at Leg-in-Boot Square. Then, if in need of refreshment, you can stop at The Riveria, a small Italian cafe where you can sit outside in the sun and taste a cafe latte or cappuccino. The pizzas here are delicious! Or if you wish, go upstairs to the charming pub, Stamp's Landing, and perhaps sit outside overlooking the marina with its colourful yachts and motor launches.

Presently, the only way back to the Market is to retrace your steps, but it is such a pleasant ride that it is not a hardship to do so. This time you will discover the scenes missed along the way. There is so much to see, that you might want to stop at one of the many benches provided and just absorb the view. **If it is Sunday, and you want to continue cycling, follow either City Tour #3 or City Tour #4,** either of which can conveniently be a continuation of this short, relaxing ride.

In the near future, cyclists will be able to follow the bicycle path around the east end of the seawall and on through the fabulous addition to Vancouver, B.C. Place, with its beautiful parks, plazas, fishing pier, commercial centres and residential areas, eventually circling back to Kits Point or continuing on to Stanley Park. This is an unforgettable trip for the whole family to enjoy.

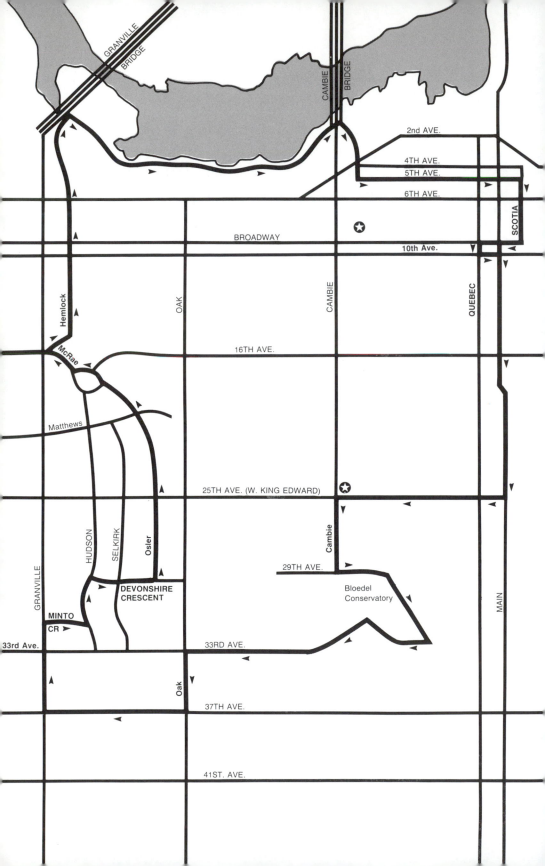

City Route #3
False Creek-Little Mountain-
Van Dusen Gardens

13 km/8 miles

Terrain: Paved road

From the east end of False Creek, at Stamps Landing, follow the path between the waterway and the apartment buildings, past the fountain at Strathern Court, turning right on Spy Glass, and cycling along the Cambie Street Bridge. Turn left under the bridge, over the tracks, bearing right on Wylie Street. There is a crosswalk on West second on Yukon Street, which you would be wise to use as this is a very busy thoroughfare. **Turn right (south) on Yukon to 5th Avenue and then turn left,** riding through a semi-industrial area of small factories and business offices. **Continue to Main Street, dismounting to push the pedestrian walk signal and cross this busy street.** You will notice that the houses remaining here are of a style popular in working class districts at the turn of the century, with their upright Victorian air and their front verandahs.

At the corner of Scotia and 5th Avenue is the impressive Indian Education Centre, which offers vocational courses to Indian youth. **Turn right (south) on Scotia, continuing to Broadway and then turn right, crossing both Kingsway and then Main Street. As you are going to turn left at Quebec from this extremely high traffic street our suggestion is to dismount and cross at the crosswalk. Cycle past the Evangelistic Tabernacle on the right side of Quebec, and turn left (east) at East 10th Avenue,** with the Mount Pleasant Baptist Church on the corner and the Ukranian Orthodox Church, with its shiny metal spires on your right.

Turn right (south) on Main Street so that you can pedal past the Dominion Agriculture Building at 16th Avenue. This heritage building, with its interesting clock tower is now a craft centre. **Turn right (west) at 25th Avenue, also called King Edward Avenue,** which is fairly wide and so quite safe for cyclists. **Turn left on Cambie Street,** at the White Spot, following this road along to **29th Avenue and then turn left (east) past the northern edge of Little Mountain. This bears to the right and changes its name to Midlothian Avenue.** On the left is the Nat Bailey Baseball Stadium, and **you are going to bear to the right, up the hill, following the signs left and then right again to the Bloedel Conservatory.** Lock up your

bicycles and visit the beautiful collection of tropical plants and tiny, colourful birds which fly freely inside the plexiglass dome. The views of Vancouver from the Quarry House and the Bloedel parking lot, which is built over the city's resevoir, are well worth seeing. The scent from the rose gardens will add to your pleasure in visiting this beauty spot. Be sure to go down into Queen Elizabeth Park, with its exotic array of flowers, trees and unusual plants.

Descend to 33rd Avenue, crossing past Holy Name Roman Catholic Church with its unique, self-supporting steel and concrete roof and then past St. Vincent's Hospital on the right and the Royal Canadian Mounted Police Building on the left. **Coast down the hill, turning left (south) on Oak Street to the Van Dusen Botanical Gardens.** The gardens are beautiful and there are often craft shows and other activities here. **Turn right (west) on 37th Avenue to the lane just prior to Granville Street. Turn right (north) parallel to busy Granville Street as far as 33rd Avenue, turning right (east) to the next lane. Turn left into the lane once more until you reach Minto Crescent. Turn right (east, bearing down to the left on Hudson.** There is a wide expanse of green at Connaught, if you are in need of a rest. **Turn right (east) of Devonshire Crescent, bearing left at the bottom along 29th Avenue to Osler Street and then turn left. Cross West King Edward** and pedal along through old Shaughnessy, with its stately homes, some of which are oldest in this first subdivision, cleared by the C.P.R. in 1909. **Follow the boulevard around the Crescent, past diplomat's mansions to MacRae and turn right to finish our combination east and westside city tour.** As you ride down the hill you will catch a glimpse of Hycroft Manor's ivy covered columns, giving you a hint of the life-style of Vancouver society at the turn of the century.

Turn right at the bottom of the hill, which is Marpole Avenue, and then left at Hemlock. After crossing Broadway, take the left lane to 4th Avenue and then immediately right to Granville Island and False Creek, where you will finish this interesting bicycle tour of just a few of Vancouver's fine attractions.

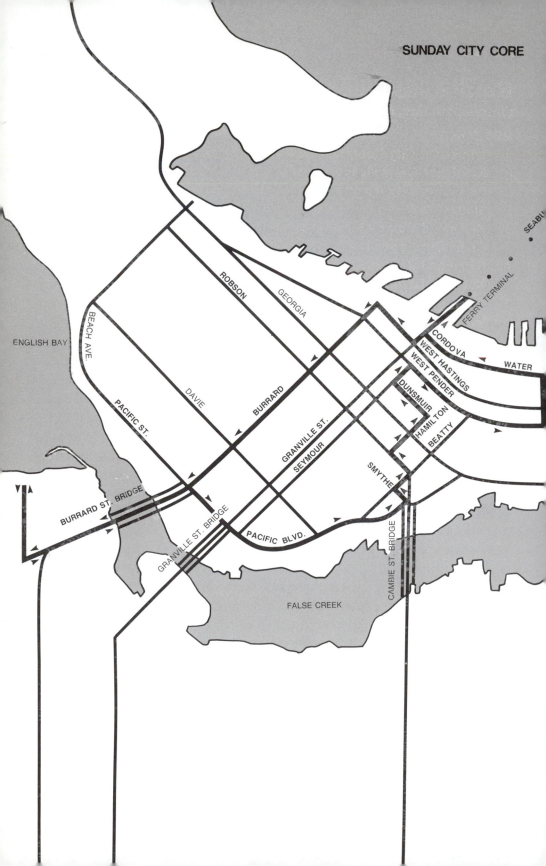

SUNDAY CITY CORE

ENGLISH BAY

FALSE CREEK

ROBSON

GEORGIA

BEACH AVE.

DAVIE

PACIFIC ST.

BURRARD

GRANVILLE ST.

SEYMOUR

CORDOVA

WEST HASTINGS

WEST PENDER

DUNSMUIR

HAMILTON

BEATTY

SMYTHE

FERRY TERMINAL

SEABU

WATER

BURRARD ST. BRIDGE

GRANVILLE ST. BRIDGE

PACIFIC BLVD.

CAMBIE ST. BRIDGE

City Route #4
Sunday City Core-Seabus-Deep Cove

40 km / 24.8 miles

Terrain: Paved roads, hilly in sections

Points of interest:
1. Terry Fox Memorial Plaza
2. C.B.C. Building on the right
3. Main Post Office on the left
4. Queen Elizabeth Theatre
5. The Dominion Building, financed by Kaiser Wilhelm, was Vancouver's first skyscraper.
6. Holy Rosary Cathedral, Vancouver's finest example of French Gothic architecture, was built with sandstone from Gabriola Island.
7. Cathedral Park is the roof of a six storey underground utilities building; three of the cylinders are air intake and the others are air exhaust.
8. Harbour Centre, with its glass elevators and magnificent views
9. The Permanent Loan and Trust Cmpany is a fine example of early temple design, used to give such an establishment an air of permanence
10. The former Sun Building, which has a copper roof and carvings of nine of the original eleven maidens, by the same sculptor who did the lions at the entrance to the Lion's Gate Bridge
11. Shanghai Alley:
    a) famous for its legal opium production until 1907, when it was outlawed
    b) the gambling and red-light district at the turn of the century
    c) old or original wooden cobbles can still be seen peeking out from under the pavement
    d) the narrowest two storey building in the world, with its underground tunnels, barber chairs and public baths. Look for the tiny spiral staircase
12. Dr. Sun Yat Sen Gardens, built by imported Chinese craftsmen and with material from China. Named after the Father of the Chinese Revolution

13. Gastown, named after Gassy Jack Deighton, who put up the first building, a saloon, in 1867. There is a statue of him, standing on a barrel of whiskey in Maple Tree Square
14. The Europe Hotel, corner of Water and Powell Streets, a fine example of the flatiron style of architecture. Visit the still elegant interior
15. Gaoler's Mews, the first gaol
16. World's first and only steam clock, heated by the underground steam heating system of a hundred buildings. On the hour it plays the Westminster Chimes of Big Ben.
17. Canadian Pacific Railway Station, with its pillared front and beautifully renovated interior. Look up at the paintings, done by Adelaide Langford in 1916, which portray scenes of the rockies.

This interesting route fits in with the Seabus schedule which only permits bicycles aboard on Saturdays and Sundays and the ride is safer on Sunday, as there is less traffic in the downtown area on this day. Take your swim suits on this trip!

Begin the ride at the south end of the Burrard Street Bridge. You may want to connect this ride with one of the other routes which begin and end at Kits Point.

If you stop briefly in the centre of the bridge you will see Expo 86 to the east and across False Creek, Granville Island framed by attractive condominiums and apartments, which hug the southern hillside. To the west are the soaring towers and highrises of English Bay.

Bear right as you exit the bridge on to Pacific St. Continue under the Granville Street Bridge entry ramp along and on down past EXPO86. **Bear left past this unusual development,** which will be used by EXPO through 1986, but which is the site of another spectacular inner-core community in Vancouver. 37% of this land will be used for parks, open spaces, seawall walks and public facilities. There will be tree-lined streets and bicycle paths, hotels, and commercial construction. The seawall will eventually connect with False Creek on the south and finally with the Stanley Park seawall, making yet another fine bicycle route for everyone to enjoy.

You are now riding directly towards the white teflon dome of The Stadium. **Turn a sharp left just after passing under the ALRT elevated train and then left on Taylor and right on Beatty. (1) Turn left on Robson (2) right on Hamilton (3,4,5) and left on one way Dunsmuir Street (6,7).**

Turn right on one way Seymour Street (8) and then right on West Pender (9).

You are now heading down the hill (10) towards the second largest Chinatown in North America, which was settled in 1858 during the Gold Rush and again during the 1870's, when the Chinese were brought into Canada as cheap labour to build the railway.

Stop for a moment at Shanghai Alley (11). It was from here that the Asiatic Exclusion League led the infamous riot on Chinatown. Visit the unique Sun Yat Sen Gardens (12).

The corner of Columbia and Pender would be a good place to lock your bicycles to a post and leave them to visit this vibrant ethnic city within a city, returning to continue to Gastown. Take the time to walk up one side of West Pender, crossing Main Street and go as far as Gore Avenue, returning to your bicycles by way of the other side of the street. **On your bike once more, turn right (north) on Columbia, travelling towards Gastown. Cross East Hastings the original main shopping street in Vancouver's early days.** These old buildings in the original downtown area were built to serve and outfit the men who were heading for the Klondike to make their fortunes.

Turn left on Water Street. You are now in Gastown (13,14). You might want to lock up your bikes and wander at your leisure through this historical part of Vancouver. Be sure to visit Gaoler's Mews (15) as well as the many souvenir shops where you will find beautiful carved Indian masks and eskimo artwork.

Continue along Water Street, so named because at that time the north side of the street was at the high tide line. The houses and Gassy Jack's saloon, shaded by wide verandah's and maple trees and surrounded by gardens, faced the shore. This was later filled in by the C.P.R. for construction and the railway tracks (16). **Continue on through Gastown, and then bear right on West Cordova,** towards the C.P.R. Station (178).

The Sea-bus is the only harbour ferry service in North America and offers both the commuter and the tourist a fast, safe, 12 minute ride to the north shore of Vancouver. Presently, bicycles are only permitted on the Sea-bus on Sundays. The fare is $1.00 per adult and you must obtain a ticket for your bicycle as well. Large picture windows afford a wide, sweeping view of both harbour activity and the city shoreline.

Exit from the Sea-bus riding up to Esplanade where you will see the

Lonsdale Quay, an extensive waterfront development, which will offer residential, commercial and recreational facilities. **Ride to the right (east) on Esplanade, crossing Lonsdale. Then bear right along the flat Low Level Road,** which will take you and any train buffs in your party directly beside the B.C. Railway tracks and then along past the Alberta Wheat Pool elevators. Continue past the Tilford Gardens, which you might want to stop and visit on the way back. **After Mountain Highway, be sure to ride in the left lane towards Deep Cove. You are now on Riverside Drive and heading over the Seymour River.** (Turn left at Seymour River Road to the delightful Maplewood Farm for children, especially at spring lambing time).

Continue bearing right on Dollarton Highway, which will take you through the Burrard Indian reserve, with its old cemetery. After leaving the reserve, descend the long steep hill, gaining speed past the Matsumoto Ship Yards to climb the other side, finally arriving at Cates Park. Here you will find tables for a beachfront picnic, washroom facilities, and nature trails through the woods.

At Dollar, the road beside the Dollar Shopping Centre, **turn right** for a quick, safe side route through an attractive residential part of Deep Cove. **Take the second left at Beachview to Mount Seymour Parkway, turning left and finally turn right at Deep Cove Rd. From this point there is a steady descent, taking you past Myrtle Park and down into this charming cove.**

For a change of pace you might want to hike a short section of the Baden-Powell Nature Trail, as far as Turtle Rock, which overlooks Deep Cove and Indian Arm. The trail goes over Seymour, Grouse and Hollyburn Mountains to Horseshoe Bay and was built in sections by the Boy Scouts. To do this, turn left at Panorama and cycle to the end, leaving your bicycles locked there. In the cove you will find a few small restaurants and boutiques to visit and if you want to explore the waterway, turn right just before the short dock and rent a canoe at a reasonable rate. Be careful! This water is dangerously cold to the uninitiated!

To return to the Sea-bus, retrace your route as far as Mount Seymour Parkway and then turn right up the hill, along the ridge and down the other side to Riverside Drive, turning left and then right again at Dollarton Highway, bearing left at the Low Level Road back to the Lonsdale Quay and on to the Sea-bus for the return trip across Vancouver inner Harbour.

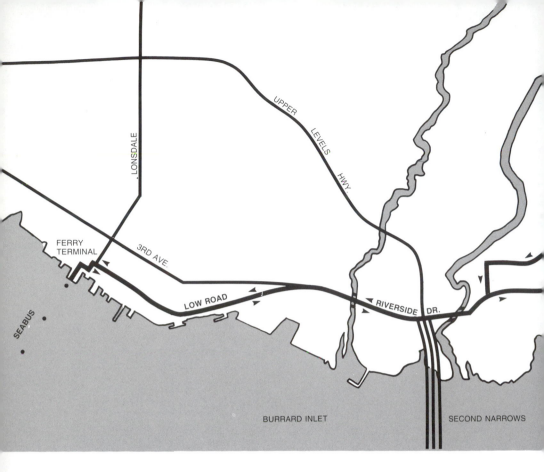

Return Points of Interest:

1. Granville and Hastings Streets (north-west corner) — Old Post Office, now to be an extensive shopping mall, a good example of Edwardian Baroque style
2, Bank of Commerce (south-east corner) Early temple style, designed by the architects of the Parliament Buildings in Ottawa
3. Marine Building, Art Deco style, 1931. Take the time to examine the detailed Terra Cotta carvings and the inlaid panelled elevators
4. Burrard Street was skid road, made of horizontally placed logs, down which trees were sent sliding from the forest above to the water below
5. 35 storey Park Place with its copper rose windows and delightful inner city park
6. Christ Church Cathedral
7. Chateau style Hotel Vancouver, which was completed in 1929, four

36

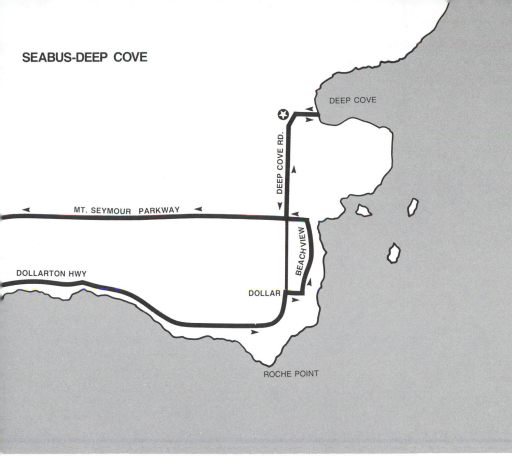

days before King George VI arrived to be one of the first guests.

8. Old Courthouse, now the Art Gallery (to the left one block) Designed by Rattenbury who designed the Parliament Buildings in Victoria, B.C.

9. Tourist Bureau and Robson Street Complex

10. Robson Street shopping area and fine restaurants

After exiting the C.P.R. Station, head up Granville Street to Hastings (1,2). Turn right, (west) on West Hastings and ride towards the Marine Building (3). **Turn left (south) on Burrard Street (4,5,6,7) to Georgia. Continue along Burrard Street to Robson (8,9,10).**

The last part of this route will take you south on Burrard Street past two turn of the century churches (11, 12). Coast south to the Burrard Street Bridge and back to your starting point. We hope you enjoyed this ride as much as we did!

City Route #5
Stanley Park

12 km / 7 miles

Terrain: paved bicycle path, flat
Stanley Park Bike Rentals: Georgia Street Entrance (1950 West Georgia)
  Ride only in an anti-clockwise direction and obey the "walk bike" signs. Take your swim suits!
  *This very special cycling tour can be connected to Routes #1,2,3,4, from the south end of the Burrard Street Bridge, by following Beach Avenue to the left (west) and, riding along beside English Bay to the entrance of the park. If you do this, you will be able to return via AQUABUS FERRY, located under the Burrard Street Bridge, to Granville Island. It is the only ferry service across the bay that will accommodate bicycles at this time.
  *Alternate Route: 15 km Park Drive, a ring road, which encircles the park, counter-clockwise, with slow moving traffic, some hills.
  *Interior paths are hard pack and paved
  The tour begins at the north-west end of Beach Avenue. Take the path to the right between the Vancouver Parks Board building, set in beautiful flower gardens, and the last apartment building on Beach Avenue. Pedal along under the shade of Beech and Alder trees to **Barclay and Lagoon, turning left immediately on Lagoon and then bearing right on the bicycle path down past Lost Lagoon.** Be careful of the geese! **Cross the bus loop, bearing left down the slight incline and under the bridge. As you come up the other side, bear left.** Pass Tudor style Vancouver Rowing Club, with the Bayshore Inn in the background.

  To the left, up the grassy slope, are two statues: the first is one of Robert Burns, the Scottish poet and the other, a little farther back is of Lord Stanley, Governor-General of Canada, who, in 1889, had the foresight to dedicate this thousand acre park for future generations. "To the use and enjoyment of people of all colours, creeds and customs for all time, I name thee Stanley Park."

  Cycle past the zoo and aquarium on the left and then the Royal Vancouver Yacht Club on the right, finally approaching Deadman's Island, now H.M.C.S. Discovery, a naval base. To the left is the Brockton Pavillion, set back on the wide, green cricket pitch, with Totem Park next to it.

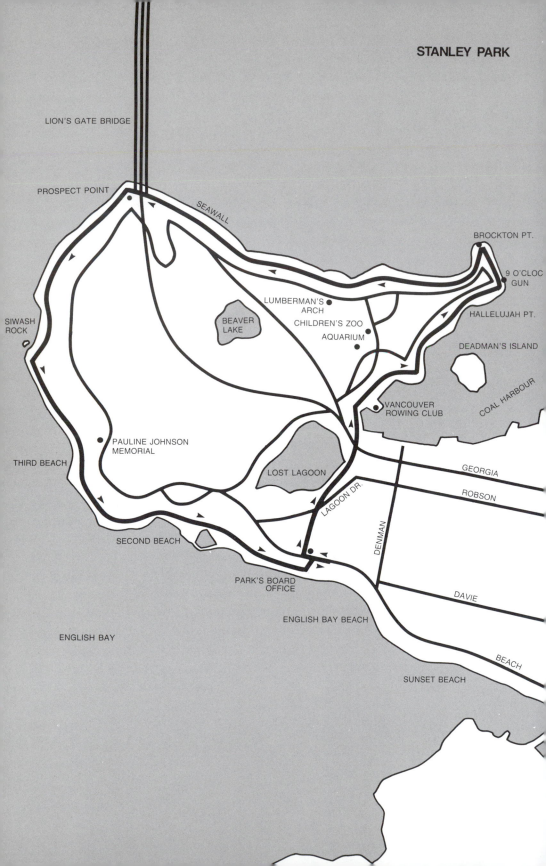

STANLEY PARK

LION'S GATE BRIDGE

PROSPECT POINT

SEAWALL

BROCKTON PT.

9 O'CLOC
GUN

SIWASH
ROCK

LUMBERMAN'S
ARCH

BEAVER
LAKE

CHILDREN'S ZOO

AQUARIUM

HALLELUJAH PT.

DEADMAN'S ISLAND

VANCOUVER
ROWING CLUB

COAL HARBOUR

PAULINE JOHNSON
MEMORIAL

THIRD BEACH

LOST LAGOON

GEORGIA

ROBSON

SECOND BEACH

LAGOON DR.

DENMAN

PARK'S BOARD
OFFICE

DAVIE

ENGLISH BAY BEACH

BEACH

ENGLISH BAY

SUNSET BEACH

Just before you ride past Hallelulia Point and the nine o'clock gun, you will have a superb view of the Vancouver skyline, with the white sails of Canada Place standing out against the blue sky. At Brockton Point you might see some of the many fishermen on the seawall catching dinner for their families, and across the harbour, at the foot of the mountains, you will see the huge piles of yellow sulphur, ready for export.

Stop to look at "Girl in a Wetsuit", captured in bronze, and sitting serenely on a rock, surrounded by ocean waves. Next you will see a replica of the bowsprit of the Empress of Japan, a ship which plied these waters from 1891-1922, carrying Vancouver's products to the orient.

Lumberman's Arch is a beautiful picnic area leading up to the Children's zoo and aquarium. The rows of Japanese flowering peach and plum trees are a breathtaking sight in the springtime. There are concessions and washroom facilities here for your convenience, as well as a map showing interior park trails. **The path now takes you under the Lion's Gate Bridge,** which offers the rider an unusual perspective of this beautifully designed suspension bridge. Prospect Point on the cliffs above is one of Vancouver's most spectacular viewpoints, and it is on this historic spot that Lord Stanley dedicated this park. The ceremony took place on "Chay-thoos", the Coast Salish word for "high bank", and the very place where Chief Khahtsahano was first interred. As you round the point, look up and see the cormorants and seagulls, nesting in the rocks.

Skaters, joggers and pedestrians share this refreshing and view-filled path with you as you head for Siwash rock, a legendary landmark. On a windy day the waves will crash against the wall and sometimes right over the top, adding excitement to this enervating ride. **The white sandy shore of Third Beach** is a favourite place for Vancouver sun worshippers, and there is a concession and washrooms on the road above. Between this beach and the next, just off this road, in a fern-filled glade, stands a small stone monument to Pauline Johnson, "Tekahionwake". This internationally known Indian poetess captured the spirit of the Indians as well as that of fledgling Vancouver, in her book, "Flint and Feather". **Continue to Second Beach,** which has a large sea-water pool, concessions, washrooms, playing fields and children's playground. **The last leg of this wonderful bicycle ride takes you up the short incline, past the Stanley Park Pitch and Putt to the end of the route.***

RICHMOND

Embraced by the three arms of the Fraser river, Richmond's three fertile islands, Iona, Sea Island and Lulu island, are a recreational cyclist's dream. In just minutes from the downtown core of Brighouse, you can be cycling down pastoral farm roads, or along the well maintained dyke trails, bordering both river and ocean. These bird infested foreshore and sand bars, delight not only the cyclist but the birdwatcher and fisherman alike. Perhaps, in season, a strawberry, raspberry or blueberry picnic, or a tour of a heritage fishing village is your cup of tea. A short drive from Vancouver, Delta, Surrey and Washington State, Richmond had it all.

Richmond Points of Interest not included in tours.
1. Minoru Chapell Heritage building and Minouru park complex
2. Richmond nature park
   215 acres of flora and fauna unique to this area, with nature trails and nature house.
3. Transportation Museum with vehicles dating back to 1917
4. Museum of Flight and Transportation
5. Richmond Arts Centre and Historical museum
6. Gateway theatre
7. Richmond Square and Lansdown shopping malls

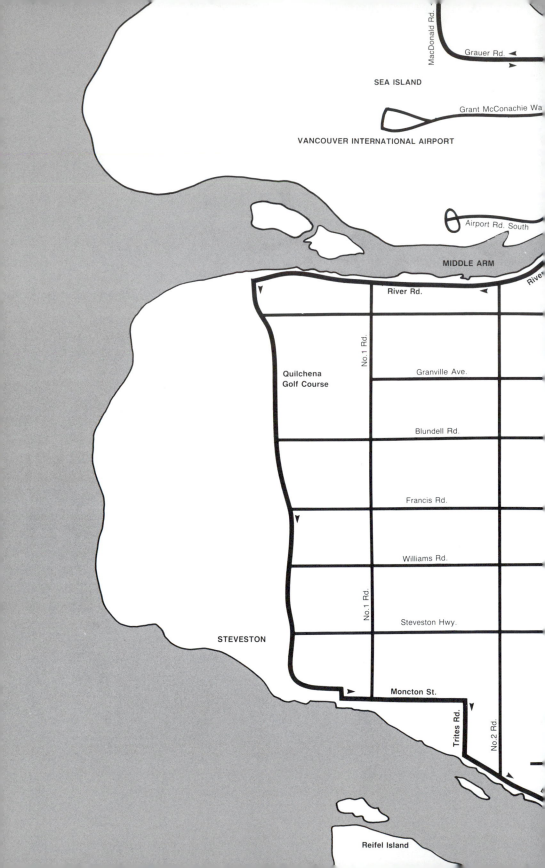

Circle Route 1
The North and West Dyke Trails

(River road to Steveston)

36 km / 22.9 miles

Terrain: Flat. Well maintained dyke trails

The tour starts at the **East** or **West Terra Nova** parking lots, situated on **River Road just west of No. 1 Road.** Both areas have adequate parking, picnic tables, benches and a great view of the airport, where at any given moment, you may see a giant 747 touch down, or disappear into the clouds. The West lot also has a public, unisex toilet.

As you turn the corner onto the West Dyke Trail there is a panoramic view of Sturgeon Banks, the North Shore mountains and the Gulf Islands. The foreshore, covered with bullrushes and sea-grass, is alive with birds of many species. Binoculars are a must!

In the fall 20,000 snow geese arrive for their Winter stopover. You will hear the cacaphony, and see a wall of white specks dipping and soaring above the water, or when at rest, an illusion of drifting snow on the foreshore.

From **Westminster Highway to Blundell,** the canal-like ditch on the left flows past the green expanse of the Quilchena golf course, and modern housing. Between **Blundell and Francis,** there are benches for the weary and there is a water tap and dish for man's best friend.

At the foot of Francis Road, there is another picnic area, with tables and trash barrels. Across the footbridge there is a large parking lot and pub.

From Francis Road to the village of Steveston, the route continues past more modern housing. Near the Steveston end of the dyke, the ditch-canal turns into a beautifully landscaped duck pond, with fountains and weeping willows. **From here the path leads (Right) to Gary point beach, or (Left) to the fishing village of Steveston.**

STEVESTON

Situated in the south-west corner of Richmond, Steveston is a thriving fishing village. First settled in the 1890's, it is now Salmon capital of the world, processing nearly 50,000,000 pounds of salmon each year.

You might wish to take a short tour of the village. Browse at Marty's Collectables, visit to one of the boutiques, or stroll through Riverside Gallery. If you want a little bit of history, the Steveston Museum is on Moncton St., in the original Royal Bank building. It has an interesting display of photographs.

Hungry? Steveston boasts many fine restaurants. If you just want a snack you might buy some fresh seafood off the boats along the riverbank, buy some fish and chips from one of the sea food take outs, or munch on some homemade pepperoni from Stawnichy's meats. If it's sweets you crave, you might try the best apple streudel in the lower mainland, at the Richmond Danish Bakery.

STEVESTON TO NO 5 ROAD

Our route continues **East on Moncton,** the main street. Cycle ast large fish canneries on the right (South) and on the left is the Steveston Martial Arts centre, the only one of its kind in North America. **Turn right (South) on Trites Road.** This will take you to the boat harbour, where draggers and gillnetters are moored at their docks, and where you may see fishermen drying and repairing their nets.

Continue (East) along the dyke where you may see freighters and sea-going tugs streaming by. Just past no. 2 road, on the left is the restored heritage farm house, London Farm. Built in 1898 by Richmond pioneers, Charles and William London, it is a reflection of pre-1900. Tours are available most Sundays from 1-4, but phone ahead to be sure. (271-3922)

Across the dyke from the farm is Gilbert Beach, popular for bar fishing and beachcombing. It is also a favorite picnic spot, so pull up a log if you've a mind to. **Continue along this scenic river-dyke trail to No. 3 Road. Turn left (North) and continue until you reach Finn Road. Make a right (East) on Finn,** past farmer's fields, where you may see the pointed straw hats of the farm workers bobbing down the rows. **Turn right on No. 4 Road. It takes you back to the dyke. Continue left. (East)**

You have arrived at Finn Slough with its picturesque floating houses and decaying boat sheds. This turn of the century boat harbour still retains some of the flavour of the Finnish fishing community, that first settled here in 1890. Photographers take out your cameras!

The route continues down the tree-lined dyke to No. 5 Road bar, another great fishing and picnicking spot. On the left side (North) of the dyke is a parking lot, picnic area and future campsite of the boy scouts and girl guides. At the north side of the parking lot is the start of the Horseshoe slough trails, a nature walk along the protected waterway, which is also suitable for canoeing.

Our circle route continues left (South) on No. 5 Road. Cycle past an industrial estate on the left and continue until we reach Steveston Highway.

Cross Steveston at the light, turn right, and walk your bike on the sidewalk until you are at the other side of the overpass. IT IS VERY DANGEROUS TO RIDE OVER THIS OVERPASS AS VISION IS GREATLY RESTRICTED! Cross back to the other side of the street and continue to No. 6 road.

NO. 6 ROAD TO TERRA NOVA

Turn left (West) on No. 6 Road. This is a quiet farm road, ideal for a leisurely ride past truck farms, greenhouses, berry and turkey farms. Continue until you get to Westminster highway. **Walk your bike across this busy street and continue down No. 6 Road till you reach Cambie Road. Turn left (West) on Cambie.** (If you have small children you may wish to walk your bikes for this part of the route, as there is heavy traffic.) **Continue down Cambie till you get to No. 5 Road. Turn right (North) on No. 5 Road. Take this route back to River Road. Turn left (West) on River Road.**

This section of the river is alive with boat traffic and industrial activity. It contrasts sharply with the tranquility of the South arm. **Turn left on No. 4 Road, right on River Drive, then veer left on Van Horne Way, left on Smith, right on Douglas, left on Sexsmith, right at Bridge-port, then left on No. 3 Road. Continue up No. 3 Road,** the last traffic-heavy portion of the route. **Turn right at Capstan Way.** The first street after the Skyline Hotel. Ride down Capstan to River Road.

Turn left on River Road. Cycle just past the Richmond Yacht club, where you may again cycle along the dyke trail.

You are now on the middle arm of the Fraser River. As you cycle along you again have a wonderful view of the airport. Boats are not allowed in this section of the river but you may see seaplanes taking off or landing. About half way down this trail at the foot of Dover Road, you come to Dover Beach. With its grass covered sand dunes, it is a pleasant picnic spot. Continue west and soon you will arrive back at **the East Terra Nova** parking lot. Our circle is complete.

Route 2
North Dyke Trail to East Richmond

24 km / 15 miles

Terrain: Flat. Paved roads

This route starts at No. 6 Road and River Road and continues to Westminster Highway.

Turn right off No. 6 Road and follow the dyke along the scenic North arm of the Fraser. The route is dotted with islands, fishing bars, and a picturesque railway bridge. At the end of the dyke trail you have the option of **backtracking to our starting point or returning via the busy Westminster highway, turning right at No. 6 Road, then back to our starting point.** This is a very easy, but worthwhile ride, if you have limited time to spare.

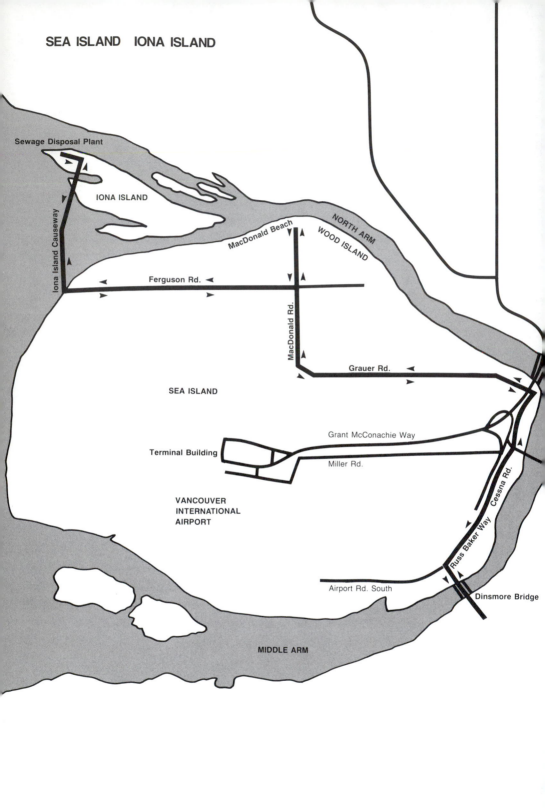

Route 3
Sea Island, Iona Island Trails

24.7 km / 15.3 miles

Terrain: Flat. Paved roads

SEA ISLAND, McDONALD BEACH

From the Dinsmore bridge follow the boat launch ramp sign to **Grauer Road. Follow Grauer till you get to McDonald Road. Turn right on McDonald and continue down to the river's edge. You are at McDonald beach * Here at riverside, there are picnic tables, washrooms, boat launch facilities and a sandy beach.** There is also a great view of the river and the lavish residential area on the other side. (S.W. Marine and environs). If you wish to fish, there is a bait concession stand here as well.
*SWIMMING IS PROHIBITED

IONA ISLAND

Backtrack from McDonald beach, south on Mcdonald Road till you come to Ferguson Road. Turn right on Ferguson. This long stretch of road passes through open fields and on the left, within yards of the airport runways. (A spectacular view of planes coming in for a landing). **Continue down Ferguson Road and across the causeway to Iona Island,** where the region's sewage disposal plant is situated.

Bird watchers from all over North America come to Iona Island to watch the many species of birds, and at the Western end of the island there is a large sandy beach. **Swimming is prohibited** here, but it is a great spot for picnicking and beachcombing. Beach improvements are planned in the near future. **You must backtrack to the Dinsmore Bridge where the tour began.**

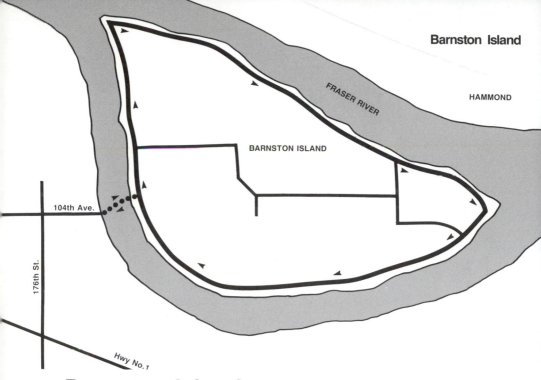

Barnston Island

12.6 km / 7.9 miles

Terrain: Flat. Paved roads

    Drive to the Eastern end of 104th Ave. Surrey to the Barnston Island Ferry dock. Park your car. * Take note that there are no public facilities on the island. Our tour starts here. The ferry runs continually from 6:20 A.M. to 11:55 P.M. every day, a short (approx.) **three minute ride to the other side.** This interesting little car ferry is really a barge, towed across the river by a tugboat that is hitched to its side. The trip, though very short, has a spectacular view of the river and the North shore mountains.

    The ferry docks at a sandy beach, and the ramp leads **to the circle island road. Turn left on this quiet country road. It is approx. 12 km full circle,** but if you wish to cut it short, **there is a cross island road approximately half way around.** The route takes you past dairy farms, booming grounds, and there are wonderful views of both river and mountains. Although most of the area is private and posed with "No Tresspassing" signs, there are areas which would be ideal for a roadside picnic. Your pastoral ride continues full circle back to the ferry. This is a neat spot for a family bike ride.

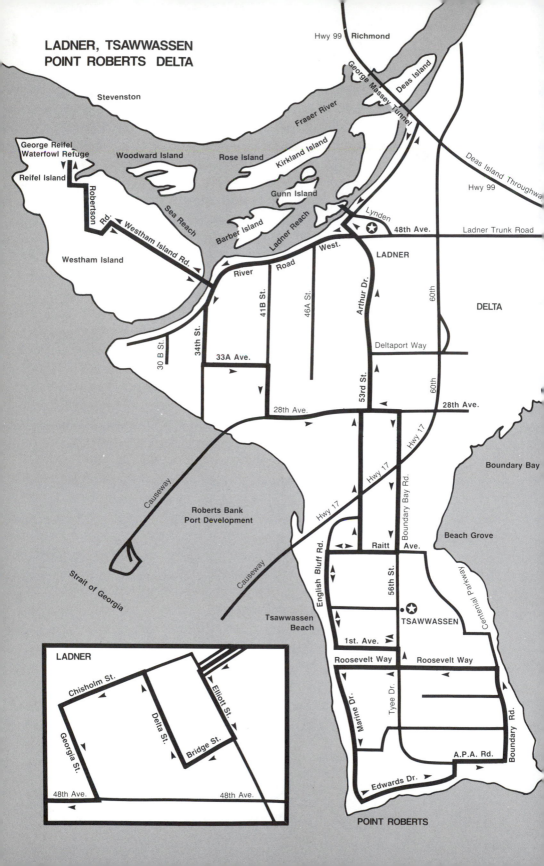

Ladner to Point Roberts Circle Tour

Including Westam Island (Reifel Waterfowl Refuge)

58 km / 36 miles

Terrain: Flat. Paved roads

Take the Ladner exit off the freeway and you will be on River Road. (If you prefer to park on the Richmond side of the tunnel, there is a free shuttle service from mid-May to end of September (Mid-May and September, week-ends only, June July and August scheduled daily service. Call Department of Highway at the George Massey Tunnel for further information. (277-2115)

It is a pleasant, tranquil drive along River Road dyke. Continue until you see a sign pointing to Ladner Park. **Turn right and park your car in the lot. Our bike tour begins with a quick tour of the park.** Ride past the tranquil lagoon, and get a fine view of the Ladner boat harbour, where hundreds of fishboats are moored at their docks. There are also picnic facilities and a playground.

Backtrack again to River Road. Continue until you get to Elliot. Take a jog left on Elliott Street, then a right on Bridge Street and cycle to Delta Street. At this point you may want to take a short tour of this quaint village with its interesting shops and many fine restaurants. Then perhaps a visit to the Delta Museum. It is a worthwhile stop. **The museum is on the corner of Bridge and Delta Streets, in the heart of the village.**

THE DELTA MUSEUM AND ARCHIVES

The Delta Museum and Archives is housed in the former Municipal hall built in 1912. As you enter you will be transported back to the time of the early settlers, stalwarts like William and Thomas F. Ladner, two of the early white settlers who arrived in 1868. As you glance into the principal rooms of a Victorian household, and walk the authentically recreated Ladner street, with its sounds of a village in its heyday, you will see how these brave pioneers carved a living out of the rich delta soil and its river abundant with fish. Recollect how these brave men and women, who despite the threat of hostile Indians, and a river that reclaimed the land each spring, survived, flourished and raised their families.

As you reach the top floor you will be transported back even further

to Delta's prehistory, the time of native settlements. For a small museum there are some good examples of Indian artifacts. There are also ship models, (a particularly good one showing the different methods of fishing showing what goes on above and below the water) ship relics and photographs of early exploration, industry and settlement.

This is a worthwhile stop to anyone interested in history and our B.C. heritage. There is also a gift shop manned by volunteers. *Museum hours are 10:00-3:30 Tuesday through Saturday. 2:00-4:00 on Sunday. Closed Monday. Admission is 50 cents for adults, 25 cents for children. (These are subject to change.)

Our route continues West on Delta to Chisholm. Then left on Chisholm. Take a short jog left on Georgia, till you get to 48th. Turn right on 48th. (Past the Belle Auberge, a fine continental restaurant). **A short jog left on 47A, then right on Stanley, which jogs left back to River Road West.** This takes you past areas of light industry, picturesque boat houses, rich farmlands, and some lovely old farmhouses which are also reminiscent of an earlier time.

Turn right across the bridge to Westham Island. Continue along Westham Road, past more lush farmlands. October to March is a good time to visit this area, as the snowgeese arrive for their winter stopover. During this time of the year, as you approach Robertson road and the Reifel Sanctuary, the fields are covered with these elegant white birds. It is a good opportunity for a close up look at these wonderful creatures, and you will be astounded by their sheer numbers. Jog right on Robertson Road, and follow it to the bird sanctuary.

GEORGE C. REIFEL MIGRATORY BIRD SANCTUARY

There are three miles of walking paths in the refuge, with 230 species of birds known to occur.

The Sanctuary is open 7 days a week from 9-4, and for a small fee you may walk through the grounds. Guided group tours can be booked ahead of time. Call 946-8546. There are picnic tables and washroom facilities as well.

Our tour backtracks to River Road West, turn right and continue past Canoe Pass Floating Village, an interesting houseboat community. Continue on to 34th st (Mason Rd.). **Jog left on 34th and continue until you reach 33A Ave. (Lewis Rd.). Turn right onto 33A and continue to 41B Street. Turn right on 41B. Ride along until you get to 28TH (Mathe-**

son Rd.). **Turn left. Continue along, following the jog left at 48th to Morley Road. Continue until you reach 56th. Turn right on 56th.** This road takes you into the heart of Tsawwassen, and is the only traffic congested portion of the tour.

TSAWWASSEN, POINT ROBERTS

Tsawwassen is a bedroom community of Vancouver, with fine shopping centres and many beautiful homes. **Our route turns right at 12th Ave., and continues down this residential street to English Bluff Road. Turn left on English Bluff.** Along this street are palacial homes, clinging to cliffs, that command a fabulous view of the Gulf islands. **Turn left on 1st Ave. and ride back to 56th. Turn right on 56th and ride on to the Point Robert's border crossing.**

Between the Canadian and U.S. border crossing is Roosevelt Way. Check in with the U.S. customs and then back up and turn right along Roosevelt Way. This road eventually connects with Marine Drive which is part of our circle tour. Veer left on Marine and continue down this wooded drive. On the left you will come to "The Roof", a boutique, art gallery and restaurant renowned for its wonderful desserts. **Our tour continues to Edwards Drive. Cycle along Edwards, past the Cannery and Reef,** dinner-dance facilities, popular with lower mainland residents. Continue on to Lighthouse park, with its great view of the Gulf and San Juan Islands. There are picnic facilities and restrooms.

Continue along the A.P.A. road to Boundary Bay Road. Boundary Bay is a popular Summer resort with sandy beaches reminiscent of Cape Cod. Unfortunately many of the shops and concession stands are closed in the Winter. **Continue up Boundary Bay Road back to Roosevelt Way. Turn left and cycle back to 56th Street and the Canadian Border crossing.**

Turn right on 56th and after a check with Canadian Customs, back to 1st Ave. **Make a left on 1st, then back to English Bluff Road. Turn right and continue till you get to Raitt. Turn right on Reitt, (12th Ave.) then left on 52nd. (Imperial Rd.)** An invigorating ride down the hill and back **across Highway 17.** On the left you will see a short lane leading to Splashdown water park, with its myriads of water slides, concession stands, and an R.V. parking lot.

Continue till you get to 28th. (Morley Rd.) Turn right onto 28th, then left on 53rd. Continue along 53rd and it soon turns into Arthur Drive. Cycle down this street to 48th (Ladner Trunk Road). Turn left at 48th and right onto Elliott, then back to River Road. Turn right and pedal back to Ladner Park.

DERBY REACH
FORT LANGLEY

WHONOCK

ER RIVER

GLEN VALLEY

264th St.

88th Ave.

272nd St.

MISSION

MATSQUI

Harris Rd.

Townshipline Rd.

Olund Rd.

Bates Rd.

Trans Canada Hwy.

Mt. Lehman Rd.

ABBOTSFORD

Fraser Hwy.

ALDERGROVE

Ross Rd.

Mt. Lehman Rd.

Peirdonville Rd.

AIRPORT

ALDERGROVE BELLINGHAM HWY.

8th Ave.

Huntington Rd.

Derby Reach-Langley Heritage Circle Tour

80 km / 50 miles

Terrain: Some gently rolling hills but mainly quite flat. Paved roads.

Drive out the No. 1 (Port Mann) Freeway to 200th Street turnoff. Drive north on 200th to 96th Ave. Turn right on 96th and drive to 201st Street. Turn left on 201. Continue North until you reach 102B Ave. Turn right. Then take a left on 208th Street and continue until you get to Allard Crescent. Take a right on Allard and continue on until you Get to Derby Reach Provincial Park. If you are planning an overnight or week-end stay, it is a good idea to set up your camp right away, as this is a very popular place, especially in summer.

DERBY REACH

This delightful little park on the banks of the Fraser, has facilities for picnics as well as overnight camping. The picnic tables and campsite pads all border the sandy beach, looking over the flowing Fraser, Haney on the other side, and a wonderful view of the mountains. There is plenty of parking space, a covered barbeque pad, water and lots of toilet facilities. In the woods, which are surrounded on one side by a split rail fence, there are sawdust trails, great for a leisurely walk. Also Derby Reach sandbar is a favorite spot for fishermen, so pack along your expandable rod. This is a self-registration campsite, with a two night (three nights on holiday weekends) time limit, and a small fee. Pets are allowed but must be kept on a leash.

Our bike tour starts as you turn left (East) on Allard Crescent, which continues along the river. Proceed to the Fort Langley monument on the left side of the road. It reads:

THE ORIGINAL FORT LANGLEY WAS BUILT HERE IN 1927
JAMES McMILLAN IN CHARGE
THE SITE OF THE FIRST PERMANENT SETTLEMENT AND CULTIVATION OF THE SOIL IN THE LOWER FRASER VALLEY
LATER KNOWN AS DERBY REACH
HOME OF THE ROYAL ENGINEERS
1858-1859

Continue through rolling hills and picturesque farms, **bearing left past golf course, this turns into 96th ave. Turn left on Glover Road (towards Albion Ferry). You are in Fort Langley.** On the left is a lovely old, refurbished community hall and the street is lined with antique, and craft shops. **Turn right on Mavis Street,** which leads you past more craft and antique shops. **Then right again on Hudson Bay Road, you will come to the B.C. Farm Machinery Musuem, Centennial Museum and National Exhibition Centre, and last but not least The Fort, the first capital of B.C.**

FORT LANGLEY HISTORIC PARK

Originally Fort Langley was part of a network of trading posts established by the Hudson's Bay Company. In 1839 the original fort, then in disrepair, was abandoned in order to facilitate a farming operation. Another fort was built 4 km up river, which was close to a large area of fertile land. Ten months after it was built, the new fort burned down. In May 1840 construction began on a new complex. The present reconstruction is built on this site.

For the next two decades, wheat production increased, beef and pork were salted for company ships and two dairies were kept in full production. The fort was also a Salmon saltery, whose products were shipped as far away as the Hawaiian Islands. Also cranberries traded by the Indians were packaged here and sent as far as San Francisco. In 1858 Fort Langley became world famous as a starting point for the Fraser gold rush. Selling mining tools and provisions became very lucrative for the company.

In August 1858 the British government revoked the licence of the Hudson's Bay Co. The "Big House" at Fort Langley hosted the ceremony proclaiming the establishment of British government on the Pacific mainland, and Fort Langley as the first capital of B.C. James Douglas, then manager of the Fort and, Governor of Vancouver Island, became the first Governor of British Columbia. Later the capital was moved to New Westminster and the traffic through Fort Langley wained.

The farm was subdivided and lots were sold. After this, the Fort fell into disrepair and in 1886, was closed. In 1955, to celebrate the Centennial of B.C. Fort Langley became a National Historic Park ad the restoration of the Fort began.

LANGLEY NATIONAL EXHIBITION CENTRE

One of the 25 exhibition centres across Canada, associated with the National Museum, it provides public access to historical, scientific and artistic exhibits. The hours are: In Winter Tues to Sat. 10 to 5, Sunday 1 to 5, Summer 7 days a week 10-5 (subject to change)

B.C. FARM MACHINERY MUSEUM

An interesting and educational exhibit of early farm machinery.

To get back on course turn right (East) on River Road, where your view is one of a tranquil river, majestic mountains and fields of grazing farm animals. To the south, you will see the tall peak of Mount Baker. **Continue till you reach 272 Street. Turn right. (South) across the valley floor** to a long stretch of wooded hills. After this long winding climb, you enter an area of gently rolling hills and picturesque farms. As you continue the road bears left, parallel to the freeway. Here you get a head on view of Mount Baker. **Bear left again and the road turns into Townshipline Road. Continue along Townshipline till you come to Mt. Lehman Rd.* Turn right (South) at Mt. Lehman Road.** This is a fairly busy street, but is wide and safe for cycling.

Proceed to Peirdonville. (At this point, if you are an airplane buff, a quick sidetrip to the **Abbotsford Airport** may be worthwhile. Just follow the signs.)

Back on track **turn right (South-West) and follow this scenic road to Ross Street. Turn left (South) on Ross, then right (West) on Huntington.** It is a busy street, but has a bike lane. As you proceed along Huntington, you will come to **Aldergrove Lake Park** on the left.

ALDERGROVE LAKE PARK

This provincial park consists of a forrested area, surrounding a sandy beach and swimming hole. It has playing fields, picnic tables, a 30 minute nature trail and a large parking lot. This park is very busy in the summer. There are no lifeguards in the park and no pets are allowed on beach area. It is open 10 a.m. to 9 p.m.

Continue down Huntington Road to 264th. Turn right and continue past Fraser Highway. **As you proceed up 264th, on the left you will see Vancouver Game Farm. It is 120 acres of farmland and forest, where live animals from all corners of the world are housed in large paddocks. It is an interesting and educational stop on the tour.

Continue along 264th across freeway overpass and continue to River Road. Turn left and backtrack to Derby Reach.

Matsqui Alternate*

23 km / 14.5 miles

If you turn right here on Mt. Lehman and again at Harris road you may take a detour to Matsqui. **Proceed to Harris Road. Turn right. Continue along Harris to Riverside. Turn left on Riverside into the village of Matsqui.** Tour around if you like, then backtrack and **proceed south on Riverside.** On the left after you pass out of the village is Wong's, a very good fruit and vegetable stand. **Continue your ride south on Riverside to Townshipline Rd. then turn right (West). Continue on and turn left (South) on Bates. Then right on Olund. Bear right up the hill out of this lush farming valley and continue on Olund until it converges with Hawkins. Follow Hawkins (Westerly) to Mt. Lehman Rd. and you are back on the main route. Turn left.**

Here you may want to turn right for a short tour down this very busy road to Aldergrove. It boasts shops, restaurants and a German delicatessen called Stoelting, famous in the lower mainland for its home-made sausage. It is on the left (South) side of the street. **Backtrack to 264th street and turn right (North).

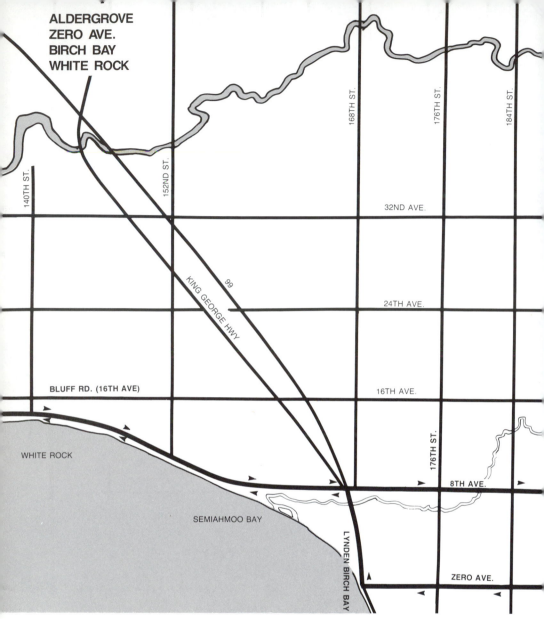

189TH ST.

176TH ST.

184TH ST.

140TH ST.

152ND ST.

32ND AVE.

KING GEORGE HWY

99

24TH AVE.

BLUFF RD. (16TH AVE)

16TH AVE.

WHITE ROCK

176TH ST.

8TH AVE.

SEMIAHMOO BAY

LYNDEN BIRCH BAY

ZERO AVE.

Aldergrove-Zero Avenue-Birch Bay-White Rock

46 km / 28 miles

Terrain: paved road, gravel stretches, a few hills

This is an excellent circle tour with the reward of a ride on the Pacific Water Slide in Birch Bay half way around, so take your bathing suits! If

70

you want to start this trip after a hearty breakfast, the Alder Hotel coffee shop provides the best bacon and eggs! Camera buffs, be ready!

Using the village of Aldergrove as a starting point, ride west to 264th Street and turn left (south) along a busy, paved road, towards the Canada-U.S. border. It's a heavy truck traffic route, but the street is wide and has a line separating the shoulder of the road from the main highway, thus it offers some protection from passing motorists and trucks.

Just before the border, bear right at the 264th Street sign and coast down the long, winding hill past tidy, picturebook farms. **You are now**

71

cycling along the little known Zero Avenue, which is a narrow country lane on the 49th parallel and the longest, unmanned border between any two countries in the world. You are riding along in Canada, with the United States of America on your immediate left (south). In the distance the American farms and silos stand out on the horizon, with the cows grazing in the foreground and on your right (north) the Canadian landscape stretches out beside you.

The road becomes wider, now with two lanes, and winds through deeply wooded areas full of small wildlife. There are some short gravel sections with sudden views between the trees of duckponds and cattle grazing in front of perfectly groomed farms. Langley has the highest deer population in British Columbia and you and your party could come across fourteen or fifteen of these beautiful creatures crossing the road at any given time.

At 213th Street there is a fairly steep hill, leading to a quaint little house made of round river stones. From the crest of this rise there is a panoramic view north to the Hazlemere Valley and the mountains. At the Douglas Border Crossing bear down to the right and to the left again. Turn left at 176th and pass through customs to "D" Street. Turn right. You are now in the U.S.A. and on your way to Blaine, Washington. **Bear left under the overpass to Blaine's main street, Peace Portal Drive.**

Blaine is a small border town with an extensive marina on the seaside and which is fronted by numerous taverns and souvenir shops. The colourful marina sits in Semiahmoo Bay, which is named after a well-known Indian tribe and which is also the name of the original Indian trail through the forest that went from New Westminster to White Rock before the turn of the century.

Continue along Portal Way, which is not really suited to cycling, as it is only a two lane street, however, **you will eventually turn right at Birch Bay Street Park, and over the railway tracks to a more suitable road. You are now on Blaine Road and will pass the Ranch Riding Stables, bearing right at Lynden Birch Bay** past the Go-Cart Racing Grounds and on to the spectacular Pacific Water Slide, one of the largest and most thrilling of its kind. After this fun-filled interlude, **turn left (south) at Harbourview,** taking this opportunity to coast down the hill into Birch Bay, with its pebble and sand beaches, picnic tables, washrooms and fast food outlets.

Leaving Birch Bay go directly north on Harbourview, past the west side of the Pacific Water Slide. Viewing it from this angle, you will be impressed by its gigantic size. **Follow Harbourview Road and then go left on Blaine Road again, thus completing a little circle route in the U.S.A. and then passing through the Douglas border and beautiful Peace Arch Park into Canada once more.**

White Rock is your next port of call, so continue straight ahead under the overpass and then make a right-hand turn, which will take you back up over the overpass (west) and on the way to sunny White Rock. Eighth Avenue leads you in and out of this southernmost town by way of a number of quite manageable hills. Coast down the first one and get up speed for the next! You can do it!

This is a very pleasant ride, with its pretty views south over the water and the houses hugging the cliff-side to the right. The traffic moves fairly slowly and so it is relatively safe for cyclists. You will see a mix of attractive townhouses and tiny, old summer cottages, as well as the Farmer's Market which is situated in an attractive heritage building. It is open Tuesday to Sunday 10:00-6:00. Closed Mondays. Hungry? Buy a snack, perhaps some fresh crab for your picnic.

Up and down the hills to the White Rock Pier you go, past the little boutiques and fast food places, the condominiums and restaurants. Lock up the bikes and take a leisurely walk along the pier to see who has caught the biggest crab. Or jump off the end and have a swim! View the wide, white sandy beach from this vantage point. Thousands of visitors come here every summer to watch the North America Sand Sculpture Contest.

The way out of the Canadian Riviera is to double back and then continue to cycle east along Eighth Avenue, also called Campbell River Road, which will take you along the flat valley floor, past typical farms and grazing land. Although there is little traffic, most motorists tend to whizz past at the legal 60 km per hour, so pay attention!

At the end of the Hazlemere Valley, just after 192nd Street, you'll have to climb a long, steep, winding hill to Campbell River Regional Park, turning left (north) on 200th Street. If time permits, there are guided nature tours and edible plant workshops in this beautiful and still natural park.

Continue north on 200 Street to 24th Avenue, turn right to Berry (208th St.) and then left (east) on Bluff (16th Avenue). This will take you back to 264th Street, when you will turn left (north) to the Fraser Highway, and then right (east) to your starting point in the village of Aldergrove.

GABRIOLA ISLAND

STRAIT OF GEORGIA

VALDEZ ISLAND

Porlier Pass

THETIS ISLAND

Stuart Channel

Ladysmith •

KUPER ISLAND

Chemainus •

VANCOUVER ISLAND

The Gulf Islands are situated along the southeast coast of Vancouver Island, nestled in the protected waters of the Gulf of Georgia. First charted by the Spanish in the 1700's, Galliano, Gabriola, Valdez and Saturna, are among those that still bear their Spanish names. Mayne, Provost and Pender were named by the British, who arrived at a later date.

These unique islands range from shrub topped rocks to well populated agricultural communities. The climate is Mediterranean, (dry summers, moderate rainfall in winter) which attracts many tourists and retired people. The lifestyle on these largely undeveloped islands is laid back and serene. This way of life is protected by the Provincial Gulf Island Trust, which carefully controls development.

The Gulf Islands are unique in their breath-taking beauty and many varied activities such as, Scuba diving, fishing, crabbing, clamming, and digging for oysters, as well as swimming, boating, picnicking, hiking, camping and cycling. There are numerous Marine parks and some camp-gounds throughout the islands, and there are many local festivals. At these celebrations, you may sample the island cuisine, and shop for handicrafts made by the islanders.

The Gulf Islands are readily accessible by B.C. ferries, private boat or sea-plane, and they provide an all year round setting for biking holidays.

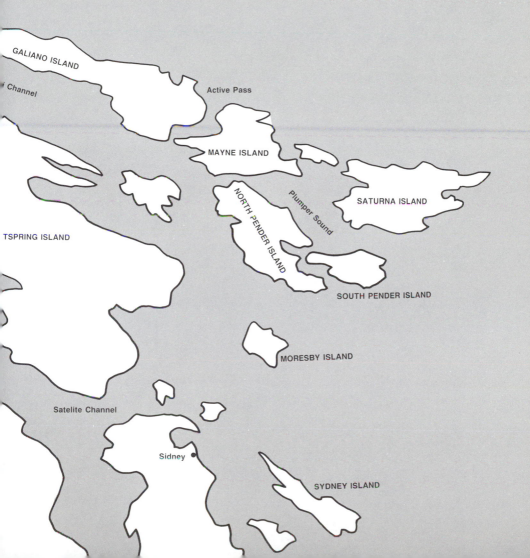

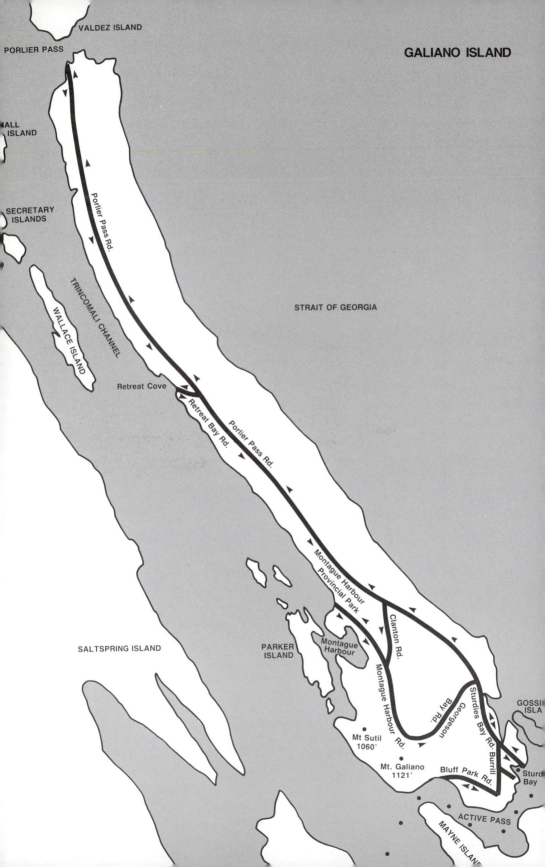

Galiano Island

72.5 km/45 miles

Terrain: Narrow, winding asphalt roads, with some loose gravel (especially Montague). Many steep hills

Galiano was first Charted in 1792 by Dionysio Galiano, commander of the Spanish squadron sent to explore this region. It is a long, narrow forested island, crowned by two peaks, Mount Galiano and Mount Sutil, the latter named after Galiano's schooner.

Take the B.C. ferry from Tsawwassen, to Sturdies Bay, or from Swartz Bay on Vancouver Island to Montague Harbour. Galiano boasts many fine restaurants, art and craft shops, stores etc., overnight accommodation and recreation areas, but this does not take away from its rural charm as it is still over 75 percent forest and bushland.

Our tour starts in Sturdies Bay. When you come off the ferry, cycle up Sturdies Bay Road, quite a long gradual hill. You will pass an information shack on the left. Here, there are maps, brochures etc., not only on Galiano and the Gulf Islands, but other areas of the province. On the right side is the "The Into Lunch Bunch", an open-air, restaurant and fish store in the back of a truck. On the first street to the left is the main street. It boasts a telephone, Dandelion art gallery, realty office and garage-come-fish store. The Dandelion is worth a stop as it exhibits and sells the works of 18 well-known local artists. At the end of this street is Galiano Lodge and restaurant.

As you continue up the hill note that bikers must keep to the right. The road is very narrow and winding, with many blind corners, and there are no shoulders to ride on. Cycle past "The Deli" on the left, up to "Burrill Bros. Store". This old fashioned country store, complete with pot bellied stove, made from an old oil can, is worth a stop. Here they sell not only groceries, whole grain breads, and delicious hand dipped chocolates, but handmade dry goods as well. In the back is a coffee and cocoa bar, where many of the locals meet, and where island intrigues go on all year long.

Our route continues past Burrill Road, past the Hummingbird Inn Pub, a local nightspot and restaurant. You will come to a fork in the road. Keep right on Porlier Pass Road. For the most part, this road is tree lined, with hills ranging from gentle, to very steep. You will pass some houses, farms and meadows and there are some interesting rock formations. **There may be some traffic, mainly large trucks so take care!**

As you continue along Porlier Road, you pass a Bakery on the left, then down the hill, be careful and watch out for blind curves. On the right you will come to Cable Bay farms. This stretch of road has a view of meadows and the odd vista of the ocean. Here the forest consists of many large arbutus trees. **Continue past the North Galiano Fire Hall, Past Madrona lodge where you get more glimpses of the water.** Then past a little Bay and beach, suitable for a picnic and swim. **Then it's up another hill, and Bodega resort on the right.**

Our route continues through a small development of attractive cottages, then you are at Critter Bay. Watch for rock on the road, just past Critter Bay. You will come to another collection of houses and end up at the Spanish Hills store. Here there is a government wharf and a good view of Trincomali Channel. You may wish to stop for a hamburger, or to pick up a souvenir t-shirt, before starting back. **(The road continues past Spanish hills store but leads to an Indian reservation, where trespassing is prohibited.)**

Backtrack to retreat Cove Road, on the right. Turn down this very narrow gravel road. (1 lane). It is a quaint country lane, taking you past meadows, a few cottages, and an abandoned farm. **At the end of the road is the wharf.** Retreat Cove is an attractive bay, sheltered by a small island at its entrance. A short walk to the left of the wharf takes you to some sandstone caves. This is another pleasant rest stop. **Backtrack to Porlier Pass road and continue to Clanton Road. Turn right on Clanton, a very good asphalt road with an interesting history.**

It seems the islanders wanted a short cut to the ferry. They petitioned the highways department. The highways's department turned them down, so they decided to build the road themselves. They were almost finished when the highways department decided it was a good idea after all, and then began to help.

Ride down Clanton Road, till you get to Montague Harbour Road. On the left hand corner is La Berengerie, a very good French restaurant. **Turn right down the hill to Montague.** Here is a marina, wharf, store for provisions and the Ferry to Swartz Bay. **Turn right, just before you reach the wharf. This gravel road leads to Montague Harbour Provincial Park.** The park provides, pleasant secluded campsites, picnic tables, toilets,

water, hiking trails and a boat launch area. There are three beaches, one at the foot of the Campsite Road (keep right at the fork). This is a gravel beach, but if you take the hiking trail on the left, or walk the sandstone foreshore you will come to a sandy beach, separated by a grassy walk from a tidal lagoon. This is a very picturesque area. Great for beachcombing, a picnic and swim.

Circle back to the fork in the road which takes you to the picnic area and boater's campsite. Here are more sylvan campsites, and at the end of the road another picnic area and beach and still another view of the bay and water's beyond.

Backtrack to Georgson Bay Road, and continue left past the corner store and Froggy's cantine. Turn right on Sturdies Bay Road and continue until you reach Burrill Road. Turn right and ride on until you reach Jack Road on the left. Turn down Jack Road and continue until you get to Bellhouse Park, a gift to the people of British Columbia by Mr. L. T. Bellhouse, May 1964. Ahead is a huge grassy bluff, which extends to a sandstone shelf on the water's edge. To the right is a stand of Arbutus trees with paths and picnic tables. At the end of the path is a small grassy point and a tiny beach. There is a panoramic view of Active Pass and Mayne Island. It is also a popular fishing spot.

Backtrack up Jack road to Burrill road. Turn left and continue, past many homes, and Penny's cottages up the hill to Bluff Park Road. This is a very rough, washboard road. Bluff park, owned and maintained by islanders has beautiful vistas of islands and sea.

On your way back on Burrill Road, you may wish to take a short detour up Shopland Road to "Earthen Things", where many of the island potters show their craft. It's well worth a stop. Backtrack to the ferry.

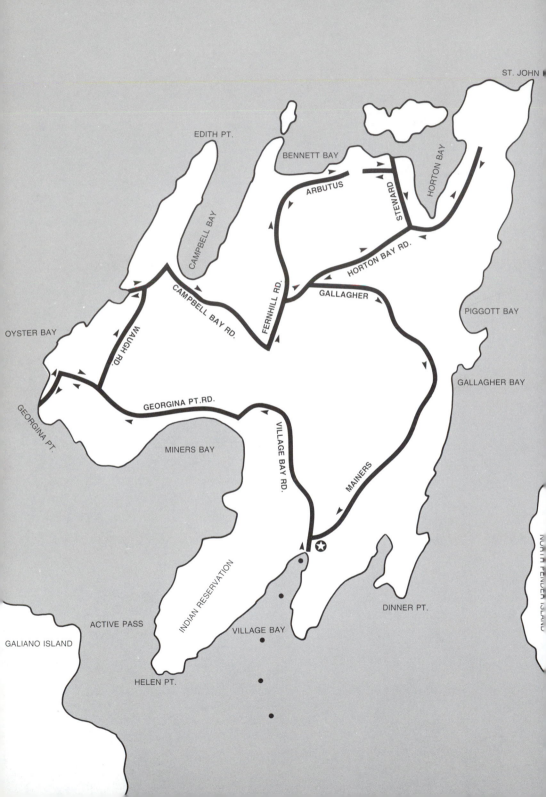

Mayne Island

ST. JOHN

EDITH PT.

BENNETT BAY

ARBUTUS

HORTON BAY

STEWARD

CAMPBELL BAY

OYSTER BAY

CAMPBELL BAY RD.

FERNHILL RD.

HORTON BAY RD.

GALLAGHER

PIGGOTT BAY

WAUGH RD.

GEORGINA PT. RD.

GALLAGHER BAY

GEORGINA PT.

MINERS BAY

VILLAGE BAY RD.

MAINERS

INDIAN RESERVATION

DINNER PT.

ACTIVE PASS

VILLAGE BAY

GALIANO ISLAND

HELEN PT.

NORTH PENDER ISLAND

Mayne Island

46 km / 28 miles

Terrain: Paved roads with loose gravel, hilly

On arrival at Village Bay you will be faced immediately with a long hill, but walking your bicycles up will give the ferry traffic a chance to pass and **then you will have a free run through a beautiful wooded section along Village Bay Road.** There are a number of Bed and Breakfast establishments on Mayne Island so you might want to make this an overnight trip. There is a delightful old museum in the small village at Miners Bay, as well as shops for supplies which you might need before you continue on to explore the island.

Turn left and then right onto Georgina Point Road, which will take you down to the lighthouse where there are daily afternoon tours during the summer months. The lighthouse overlooks the busy and sometimes treacherous Active Pass.

Backtrack to Waugh Road and turn left. This will take you around to David Cove and then on to Campbell Bay Road. This route winds along the bay beside broad grassy farmland on one side and with a fine view of the sea on the other. **Turn left on Fernhill,** which will take you past Fernhill Herb Farm, a well-known Bed and Breakfast, **and follow this down to Arbutus, bearing right to Bennett Bay.** This is a perfect picnic stop, with stony beaches and outlooks to Curlew and Georgeson Islands. One of the many small resorts on Mayne Island is located in this pretty bay. **Now you can remount and head back to Fernwood Road, turning left at Horton Bay Road. This will take you through beautiful secluded woods to the government dock for a swim or turn left on Steward** for a different view of the aforementioned islands. **Either way you will have to return on Horton Bay Road to Gallagher, turning left down to Piggot and Gallagher Bays.**

Follow Mainers for the return trip, bearing right at the fork to Village Bay Road and then left to the ferry. No ferry waits for you! As the boat slips out of the dock and around Helen Point, you can lean on the rail and admire the water view of the Lighthouse as you sail through Active Pass, and enjoy memories of wonderful bicycle outing on the Gulf Islands.

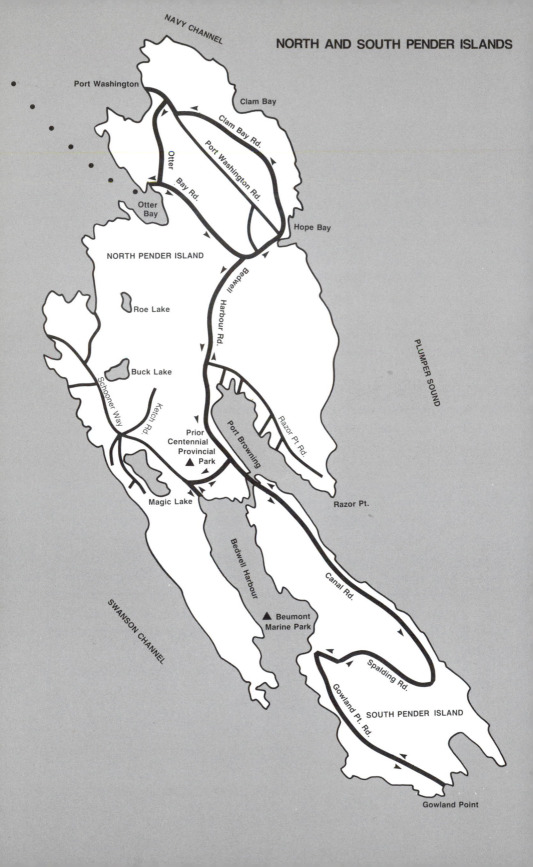

NAVY CHANNEL

NORTH AND SOUTH PENDER ISLANDS

Port Washington

Clam Bay

Clam Bay Rd.

Port Washington Rd.

Otter Bay Rd.

Otter Bay

Hope Bay

NORTH PENDER ISLAND

Roe Lake

Bedwell

Harbour Rd.

PLUMPER SOUND

Buck Lake

Schooner Way

Ketch Rd.

Razor Pt. Rd.

Prior Centennial Provincial Park

Port Browning

Magic Lake

Razor Pt.

Bedwell Harbour

Canal Rd.

Beumont Marine Park

SWANSON CHANNEL

Spalding Rd.

Gowland Pt. Rd.

SOUTH PENDER ISLAND

Gowland Point

North and South Pender Islands

41.8 km / 26 miles

Terrain: Gently rolling hills, few steep hills, paved, some loose gravel

Take the Gulf Island ferry from Tsawwassen. When you arrive at Otter Bay, cycle up the hill on Otter Bay Road. (Bikes must keep to the right and travel in single file.) This is a tranquil wooded road, forested with evergreens and Arbutus trees, and in season there are myriads of wild flowers on the roadside. The road is paved and there are many gently sloping hills.

Continue until you get to the Bedwell Harbour Road. Turn right. You will pass a firehall and police station on the right. This is an area of scenic meadows and farms and there is a graveyard on the right. The road becomes forested again as you proceed down a fairly steep, winding hill, then into another valley of green fields and farmhouses. There is a helicopter pad on the right and a little further on, a gas station-store with a take out window, and a specialty shop.

Continue along this road until you get to Prior Provincial Park. It is worthwhile taking a short tour of the park and if you are staying overnight, a good time to set up camp. The facilities here are very good, with hiking trails, wood, water, toilets and picnic tables. Although it is not near the sea, this is very picturesque setting, especially with the sun streaming through the huge trees.

Back to Bedwell Harbour Road, and continue to the Canal Bridge. Just before the bridge on the left side is a marker. It reads as follows:

Here, near this point, passes an ancient trail over which Indian portaged their canoes between Browning and Bedwell Harbours, across this neck of land. Pioneer settlers later dragged their boats on skids, for visits between the scattered island families, or to shorten the journey to Sydney by sail or rowboat. In 1903 at local request, the federal government constructed the nearby canal, dividing Pender Island.

Just past the marker, on the same side of the road, is the archeological excavation site of Simon Fraser University. It is open for tours 9:00-12:00 1:00-4:30 during the season, and tours are conducted by the courtesy of "Challenge". This is a fascinating and worthwhile stop. Who knows you may witness the discovery of some Indian artifacts. Below the site is water access.

Cross Canal Bridge, which has only one lane and a spectacular view of the canal. Just over the bridge on the left is beach access. On this side is a winding hill, with only occasional glimpses of the water. You pass some fields and farms and come to another very small and narrow valley, with neat farms and flocks of sheep. As you continue the road is lined with Arbutus trees. **Turn the corner past the Anglican Church of the Good Shepherd.** You then get glimpses of the water and come upon giant rock formations on the right. They are quite spectacular and look as if some giant hand placed them there. Definitely worth a picture. As you continue you see still more of these rock formations placed here and there alongside the road. **Keep right when Canal Road turns into Spalding and then Gowland Pt. Road. At the end of the road is Gowland Point beach, a good place to stop for a picnic and a swim.** Here is a spectacular view of Mount Baker and the islands. You might also see a friendly seal or otter.

Backtrack to the Bedwell Bay Resort sign. Turn down the hill to the resort. The facilities there include a lodge, swimming pool, restaurant, post office, and marine and pub. There are also camping, picnic facilities and fresh water at Beumont Marine park.

Go back to the junction of Otter Bay road, but this time keep right on Hope Bay Road, past attractive old farm houses and fields to Hope Bay. Here is picturesque old Corbett's store, circa, 1905. Unfortunately it is no longer open. This is where the ferries used to land.

Backtrack a little on Clam Bay Rd. Continue until you come to Port Washington Road. Turn right, down the wooded road, past farms, orchards and fruit stands (in season), to Port Washington, a scenic bay with another heritage general store. This one, circa 1910, is open. There is also an interesting looking craft shop at the wharf, but it is open only on weekends.

Backtrack to Otter Bay Road. Turn right and continue past the Pender Island Golf course to the ferry.

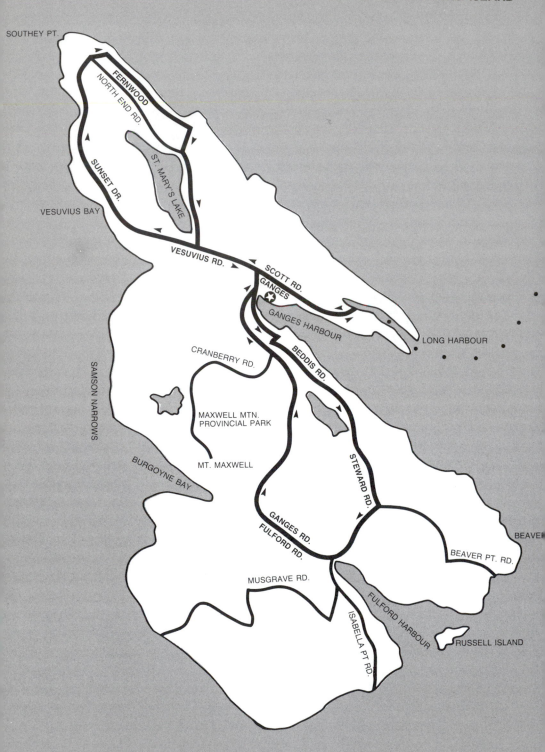

SALTSPRING ISLAND

SOUTHEY PT.

FERNWOOD

NORTH END RD.

ST. MARY'S LAKE

SUNSET DR.

VESUVIUS BAY

VESUVIUS RD.

SCOTT RD.

GANGES

GANGES HARBOUR

LONG HARBOUR

CRANBERRY RD.

BEDDIS RD.

SAMSON NARROWS

MAXWELL MTN.
PROVINCIAL PARK

MT. MAXWELL

STEWARD RD.

BURGOYNE BAY

GANGES RD.

FULFORD RD.

BEAVER PT. RD.

BEAVE

MUSGRAVE RD.

ISABELLA PT RD.

FULFORD HARBOUR

RUSSELL ISLAND

Saltspring Island

99.8 km / 62 miles

Terrain: Paved as well as rough gravel, hilly

Let the ferry traffic pass before you start!

Hardy cyclists can go for a day's challenging ride, while others may wish to stay overnight and take two days to tour this island, the largest of the Gulf Islands.

From Tsawwassen to Long Harbour is a view-filled thirty minute voyage by ferry. Arriving at your destination, you will sail down the narrow passage called Long Harbour, past many colourful yachts and motor launches. It is a beautiful introduction to Saltspring, which has the earliest records of settlement of all the islands. Look up at the attractive summer homes perched along the low bluffs as the ferry glides in. There are no eating facilities offered on this trip, so take a picnic lunch or be prepared to buy a snack in Ganges or Fulford Harbour. You will find washroom facilities in the waiting room at the ferry dock as well as in the park in the nearest village, which is a favourite shopping stopover for the boating fraternity.

South end of the island:

From Long Harbour follow the winding and hilly, tree-lined route along Scott Road, left on Fulford to the village of Ganges, where there is a farmer's market and other little shops where you can get supplies. The Mouat Provincial Park is just past Ganges on the right and has facilities for overnight camping.

Go left on Beddis Road. A side road off Beddis will take you down to a sandy spit, which is well protected from the wind and where the shallow water has been warmed by the sun. **Continuing along Beddis Road,** and just before Steward, there is a little road down to an interesting rock castle you might like to visit. **Follow Steward,** and at the next fork in the road, you might want to take a quick downhill trip on Beaver Point Road to Ruckle Farm, riding through the lush, fern-filled woods. You will see the interesting gnarled branches of the distinct, red-barked, Arbutus trees all through this area. If you plan to stay overnight, turn right at Cusheon Lake Road, and ride down Natalie Lane into delightful Cusheon Lake Resort. Rosemary and Helmut Boehringer will welcome you to their

well-equipped log cabins. They have installed an outdoor jaccuzi for their guests, and have boats for fishing as well as canoes to paddle on the tranquil waters. The lake is well stocked with Speckled Trout and Bass, so bring your fishing rods!

Fulford Harbour offers a small coffee shop whose cook makes mouthwatering muffins for your picnic. Visit the old cemetery in the churchyard on your way out of the harbour. **Bearing left on Fulford Road (also called Ganges Rd.) once more,** mountain bikers might want to try two side trips: Isabella Point Road or Musgrave Road, the latter leading to a Government dock. Great fishing here if you have the time! This part of the route is fairly hilly. Cranberry Road which leads off Fulford to the left, will take you to Maxwell Mountain Provincial Park and Burgoyne Bay, just off the famous Sampson Narrows, where the fish all but jump into your boat!

The easiest tour of the island is the north end, which interestingly is called Southey Point!

From the town of Ganges follow Fulford Road north to Scott and turn left on to Vesuvius Road. At this intersection you will pass the Saltspring Island Golf Course and tennis courts, as well as washroom facilities.

You could take a side trip right on North End Road to St. Mary's Lake and have a dip in the warm water, but **our tour continues on Vesuvius Rd. to Vesuvius Bay,** where you will find excellent seafood restaurants. From here you can take the small ferry to Crofton, on Vancouver Island.

Go north along Sunset Drive, a hilly, narrow, winding road, lined with sheep farms. **Follow this to Southey Point** where there is a trail down to the beach, **and then back along the water's edge, left and then south on Fernwood, continuing on Walker Hood Rd.** It was because of the salt springs in this area that the Indians originally named the island "Klaathem" (salt). Along this picturesque stretch of white, sandy beach you might see a bald eagle soar overhead, as we did while we were cycling slowly along absorbing the natural beauty of this island paradise.

Leaving this memorable tour behind you, **turn left at Scott Road, riding down to the ferry slip, and the end of your adventures on Saltspring Island.**

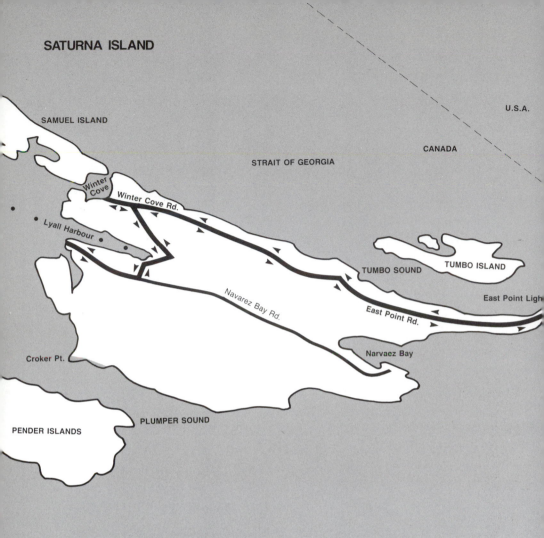

Map labels: SAMUEL ISLAND, Winter Cove, Winter Cove Rd., Lyall Harbour, STRAIT OF GEORGIA, CANADA, U.S.A., TUMBO SOUND, TUMBO ISLAND, East Point Light, East Point Rd., Navarez Bay Rd., Narvaez Bay, Croker Pt., PENDER ISLANDS, PLUMPER SOUND

SATURNA ISLAND

29.6 km / 18 miles

Terrain: Very Hilly, paved with a lot of loose gravel

Take the Gulf Island ferry from Tsawwassen to Village Bay on Mayne Island, transferring there to the Saturn Island ferry. (Please check the schedule to make sure there is a return trip that day from Saturna, as there are very few facilities on the island for overnighters.) On arriving in Lyall harbour, you will notice on the right hand side of the road, a pub, grocery store and gas pump. Continue up a steep hill past the

94

post office and fire hall, till you come to a fork in the road. **Veer left onto East Point Road.** This old lighthouse road is paved but with some loose gravel, so take care.

Our route continues through the forest, passing the occasional small farm or cottage. This part of the tour is very hilly. **When you come to a stop sign turn right.** Shortly you will arrive at a tree lined section of road, with a good view of the water, an interesting sandstone beach and a great view of the mountains. There are some huge arbutus trees here, and the terrain is fairly flat. There is an abundance of birds, both seabirds and the land variety. Keep your eyes out for the many bald eagles that live on the island. This is a good spot for a picnic and perhaps a swim.

Continue up the gently curving hills. At the fork in the road stay to the right. Here the road is very narrow, with a great deal of loose gravel, but there is virutally no traffic. As you ride you may get an occasional glimpse of Turbo Island through the trees and you will pass some very picturesque cottages. **Cycle on till you get to the end of the road, where East Point Lighthouse sits** on a grassy plateau, surrounded by a sandstone beach. This is the extreme southwestern tip of the Gulf Islands. Unfortunately the lighthouse is fenced and there is a "no trespassing" sign. **There is a dirt path to the left, which takes you down to a pebbled and sandstone beach. Walk your bike down this path.**

Take a walk on the sandstone beach, below the lighthouse. You will get a good view, not only of the lighthouse itself, but out to sea, the San Juan islands, including the U.S. Coast Guard station on Patos Island and Mount Constitution on Orcas Island. The beach itself has some interesting sandstone formations, and sea life abounds. This is another good place for a picnic and picture taking.

Backtrack to the junction of Winter Cove and East Point Road. There is a gravel road to **"Winter Cove Marine Park".** The park is situated on a scenic bay, and has picnic tables, BBQ's and campfire facilities, a forest hiking trail and toilets. However, there is no overnight camping.

Backtrack to the Lyall Harbour to the ferry dock. On the way you pass Boot Cove road on your left. Near the end of this road is Boot Cove Bed and Breakfast.

If you are there on the July 1st weekend, try and hitch a ride from a friendly boater to the annual Saturna Island Lamb Roast. It is a real event, as Saturna is famous for its lamb. It is held at Breezy Bay on private property. In the afternoon there is an old fashioned country fair, with a craft sale, games, and a beer garden followed by a lamb feast.

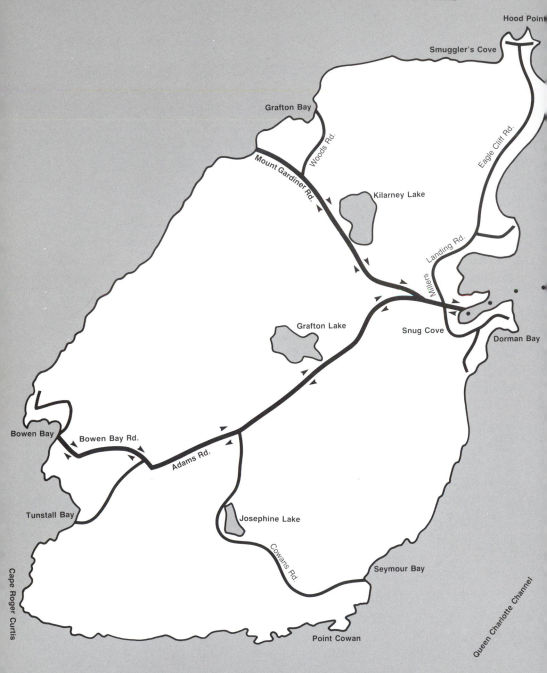

BOWEN ISLAND

Howe Sound

Hood Point

Smuggler's Cove

Grafton Bay

Eagle Cliff Rd.

Woods Rd.

Mount Gardiner Rd.

Kilarney Lake

Landing Rd.

Miller's

Grafton Lake

Snug Cove

Dorman Bay

Bowen Bay

Bowen Bay Rd.

Adams Rd.

Tunstall Bay

Josephine Lake

Cowans Rd.

Seymour Bay

Cape Roger Curtis

Queen Charlotte Channel

Point Cowan

BOWEN ISLAND

Bowen is one of the most accessible of the gulf islands. It was first charted by the Spanish, in 1791 and called "Isla de Apodoca." In 1860 it was renamed "Bowen" by the British, after Rear Admiral James Bowen The ferry trip to the island is only twenty minutes across Queen Charlotte Sound.

As you round the point leaving Horseshoe Bay, your first view is of a tree covered isle crowned by the 2500 foot peak of Mount Gardiner. As you pass into open water there is a spectacular view of Passage Island, Point Atkinson and Point Grey.

Entering Snug Cove there are many attractive summer homes on the point, and the cool smooth water in the bay is as green as the trees that are reflected in it. This cove is the only commercial area of the island and the only public restroom facilities are at the ferry dock. **Head up Government Road** and your first point of interest is the newly refurbished **Union Steamship store.** Lately saved from demolition by the Bowen Park and Store Society, with the aid of government grants, the general store, first built in 1928, by the Union Steamship Company, was moved back off the road, totally renovated and landscaped. It is situated in Crippen Regional Park, on land purchased by the Greater Vancouver Regional District. Plans are now underway to further develop this park. Nature trails, horse and bike trails, restrooms, and picnic facilities are planned.

SNUG COVE

You may wish to take a tour of the Cove. **Take a left on Cardena, just before the refurbished General Store. It leads to a placid, green freshwater lagoon on one side and Deep Bay on the other. If you continue up the little rise, there is a pleasant residential area. Circle around, then backtrack to the lagoon. Turn left on Cardena and you will come to the Sheilding Gallery, of well known artist Sam Black.** He is especially noted for his seabirds, especially seagulls. It is definitely worth a stop.

Beside the gallery is Sandy Beach, a favorite spot of summer residents and picnickers alike. **You may continue along past the C.N.I.B.'s summer residence and out to the point, past the attractive homes you spotted while entering the bay. Backtrack to the store.**

Route 1   Snug Cove-Bowen Bay

16 km/9.93 miles

Terrain: Very long steep hills at the beginning and end, but in the middle, gentle rolling hills. Paved roads

Continue up the steep government hill, past the cafe, noted for its fish and chips, a small collection of shops including a bakery that makes a delicious whole grain soda bread, (Bowen Bread) a supermarket-liquor store and small shopping mall. **Pass the Dorman-Miller crossroads (gas station on the corner)**

Once you get to the top of the government hill the route is occasionally hilly, but not strenuous. It is a tranquil ride with very little traffic, mostly forest-lined with just the occasional house, meadow or farm. **Continue past (Trout) Grafton Lake, on the right.** No swimming is allowed as it is a water reservoir. **Keep on until you get to Adams Rd. Turn right and travel along, passing Tunstall Bay Road,** which leads to a pebbled beach. **Turn right on Bowen Bay Road then down the long Bowen Bay Hill.** At the foot of the hill, by a small collection of houses, is a sandy beach and Arbutus point. This is a pleasant spot for a cool swim and a picnic. From the beach there is a good view of Paisley Island and Georgia Straight. After your respite, **backtrack to the top of Government hill.**

Route 2   Mount Gardiner

10 km/6.25 miles
Terrain: mainly gently rolling hills. Paved roads

At the school turn left down Mt. Gardiner Rd. This is another tranquil and slightly easier route. **Continue to picturesque Kilarney lake.** This once private lake is now part of Crippen Park. Some clearing has been done, to prepare for the proposed horse and bike trails. Here is another great place for a picnic and swim. **Continue through the woods till you get to a signpost (Mt. Gardiner-Grafton Bay). Follow the Mt. Gardiner route on the left. It takes you down to the government dock and a pleasant rocky beach.** Here another cool swim may be in order. Across the water is Hutt Island, and Howe sound in the distance, where you may see the Sunshine coast ferry glide by. **You must backtrack to Snug Cove.**

98

Gabriola

19.8 km/32 miles

Terrain: Paved roads, hilly

    *B.C. Ferry from Horseshoe Bay to Nanaimo: summer hours — every hour on the hour, 7:00 A.M. - 10:00 P.M., winter hours — every two hours on the hour, 7:00 A.M. - 9:00 P.M. Fare (1985) $6.00 (including bicycle). Aprpoximate sailing time, 1 hour 40 minutes.

    *Departure of Highways Ferry from Nanaimo to Gabriola: every hour, on the half hour, 6:00 A.M. - 10:45 P.M. Fare (1985) $1.35 (including bicycle). Approximate sailing time, 15 minutes.

    *Take your swim suit, your fishing rod, and your clam shovel!

    This is a manageable day trip from Vancouver, and it includes two delightful ferry trips, **starting from Horseshoe Bay in West Vancouver. Disembark at Nanaimo, following the highway signs to the city centre. Turn left at Front Street and follow this road, past the old fort to the Gabriola Ferry.**

    Board the ferry for a refreshing short trip to this 16 mile long island, where you will cycle through forest and farmland and when you're finished you can reward yourself with an ocean dip in the clean, cool waters off one of the rocky beaches.

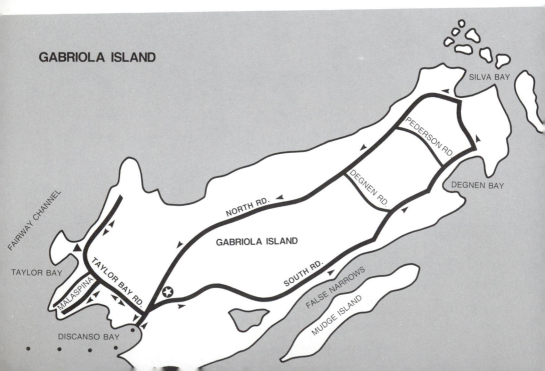

GABRIOLA ISLAND

SILVA BAY

PEDERSON RD.

DEGNEN RD.

DEGNEN BAY

FAIRWAY CHANNEL

NORTH RD.

GABRIOLA ISLAND

TAYLOR BAY

TAYLOR BAY RD.

MALASPINA

SOUTH RD.

FALSE NARROWS

MUDGE ISLAND

DISCANSO BAY

Disembark at Discanso Bay and head up the first steep hill past the White Hart Pub. At the Post Office, take the South Road, right, towards Silva Bay. Along the way you will pass one of the largest Jack-Knife clam beaches in the islands, so you might want to stop here and start shovelling! There is an excellent view of Mudge Island, and at the narrowest point in the channel there is a proposed bridge and highway route from Gabriola to Mudge to Vancouver Island. From here to Degnen Bay and on to Silva Bay you will pass charming old farms. Don't forget to stop for a minute at Gossip Corner to tell a tale of two! During the summer, as you pedal along you will be assailed by the sweetest summer scents, as well as smells of orchards and the sea. Delightful! For a change of pace, you can rent a boat at Silva Bay and perhaps do some fishing. **North Road, which will take you back to the ferry,** runs mainly through secondary forest where there are extensive riding trails. **If you have time, on your return towards the ferry slip, be sure to take a short side trip, right on Taylor Bay Road, and left on Malaspina Drive to the unusual geological formation called the Malaspino Galleries.** This is a perfect spot for a swim as you can dive in at the caves. After your swim, **continue along Taylor, turning left at Berry Point Road.** This is a beautiful, quiet road along the shore with distant views of the Sunshine Coast. You might want to stop for lunch at rustic Surf Lodge to enjoy their fine cuisine, before retracing your steps to the ferry and leaving behind this beautiful island.

Bicycle Repair Shops "En Route"

1. ALRT:
   Cap's Bicycle Stores, 420 East Columbia, New Westminster, 524-3611
   Edmonds Cycle, 7538 Edmonds, Burnaby, 522-3124
   Jubilee Cycle, 4816 Imperial, Burnaby, 434-4922
   Cuervo Bicycles, 1037 Commercial, 255-1919
2. Vancouver City Routes:
   - #1: West Point Cycles, 3771 West Tenth Avenue 224-3536
     Varsity Cycles, 4385 West Tenth Avenue, 224-1034
     Dunbar Cycles, 4202 Dunbar Street (at 26th Avenue), 738-7022
     Bicicletta, 2803 West 16th Avenue, 734-3228
   - #2: Reckless Rider Cyclery, 1650 West 1st Avenue, 738-2921
   - #3: Three Vets (supplies), 2200 Yukon Street, 872-5475
     Bikes of Broadway, 620 East Broadway, 874-4288
     Cambie Cycle, 4038 Cambie Street, 874-3616
   - #4: Robson Cycles, 1463 Robson Street, 687-2777
     North Star Cycle, 1719 Lonsdale, North Vancouver, 980-1317
     Deep Cove Bike Shop, 4322 Gallant, North Vancouver, 929-1918
   - #5: Cicli Forza, 1184 Denman Street, 669-3646
     Bayshore Bicycles, 1876 Georgia Street, 689-5071
3. Richmond:
   Richmond Cycle Centre, Park Village Shopping Centre, 6591 Buswell, 278-1555
   Richmond Rocky Cycle and Sport, 8120 Westminster Hwy., 273-4111
   Caps Cycle, 10831 #4 Road, 271-2811
   Tailwind Cycle, 136-4800 #3 Road, 273-8050
   Steveston Bicycles, 3731 Chatham Street, Steveston, 271-5544
4. Tsawwassen:
   Work Shop, 55575 16th Avenue, 934-4131
   Home Hardware, 12028 56th Avenue, 943-2701
   Delta Bicycle & Lawnmower Repair, 5064 48th Avenue, 946-9827
5. Langley:
   Bishop Cycle Shop (Reliable Cycle), 20478 Fraser Hwy., 534-3913
   Locomotion (Henry Sport and Cycle), 111202 56th Avenue, 534-4818
6. Aldergrove & White Rock:
   Henry Sport & Cycle, 1465 Johnston, White Rock, 531-8111
7. Gulf Islands:
   With the exception of Saltspring Island, use local hardware stores and service stations

Routes Listed by Degree of Difficulty
(Terrain, distance, quality of road surface)

BEGINNER
1. Vancouver City Route #2
   Kits Point-Granville Island-False Creek
2. Vancouver City Route #5
   Stanley Park
3. Richmond Route #1
   Circle Dyke Tour
4. Richmond Route #2
   North Dyke to East Richmond
5. Richmond Route #3
   Sea Island-Iona Island
6. Barnston Island
7. Bowen Island Route #2
   Snug Cove-Mount Gardiner

BEGINNER-INTERMEDIATE
1. Fort Langley-Derby Reach Heritage Tour
2. Zero Ave.-Aldergrove-Birch Bay
3. Ladner-Tsawwassen-Point Roberts
4. Mayne Island
5. Gabriola Island

INTERMEDIATE
1. Vancouver City Route #1
   Kits Point-U.B.C.-Southlands-Shaughnessy
2. Vancouver City Route #3
   False Creek-Little Mountain-Van Dusen Gardens
3. Vancouver City Route #4
   Sunday City Core-Seabus-Deep Cove
4. Galiano Island
5. Saturna Island
6. Bowen Route #1
   Snug Cove-Bowen Bay
7. North and South Pender Island

ADVANCED
1. Saltspring Island